# Petal, Leaf, Seed

## Cooking with the treasures
## of the garden

**LIA LEENDERTZ**

**PHOTOGRAPHY BY
MARK DIACONO**

# Contents

# Introduction

Have you ever infused a fig leaf in custard and had its coconut and elderflower scent waft up to you on clouds of milky steam? Or picked a handful of fennel seeds when they are still green and fat and scalded them with boiling water for a sweet, grassy, anise-scented tea? Or maybe you have decorated a salad with bright purple sage flowers, with a flavour that's deeply herbal yet honeyed? If the answer to any of these questions is no, this book will open your eyes to the hidden flavours in your garden.

Within these pages lie many overlooked delicacies that grow away unassumingly outside our back doors – a secret larder. You may even be growing many of them already. Larder may well be the wrong word here, for it implies a level of provision that fills stomachs. The petals, leaves and seeds in this book make up something more akin to a spice cupboard; conveying citrusy, floral, nutty, aromatic, sweet, tea-like, spicy, herbal and peppery hints, and many more besides. This book is not concerned with the bulky produce of the garden but its hints and wafts, and the ways in which you can unlock them to make more varied, delicious dishes.

The initial spark for this book was a failure. Several years ago I bought a peach tree and planted it in my sunniest and most sheltered spot, anticipating summers plucking peaches dripping with golden juice. The peaches never came. Or rather, one or two occasionally reached a sort of ripeness, but even they didn't taste of much. In my frustration I was on the verge of cutting it down when a friend mentioned that she had read about peach leaves themselves having a flavour. I certainly had plenty of leaves, so I went home and plucked and sniffed a few – nothing. But then I boiled them into a hot simple syrup. The strength of the sweet almondy scent was astonishing and magical. Here was a crop of flavour, not bulk, and there soon followed almond-flavoured liqueurs, pannacottas, rice puddings and ice creams. The tree stayed. The experience made me look at my garden with new eyes and wonder what other garden produce holds similar hidden depths. The results of this search and experimentation are contained in this book.

There are plenty of far more common ingredients in this book, too: petals, leaves and seeds that are well known for their ability to transform dishes from ordinary to complex and mouthwatering. The common thread here is that every ingredient is small and beautifully flavoured, rather than hefty and filling. These are the treasures of the garden, and – like the peach leaves – I have found that they are often far more dependable and easier to grow than the bulky fruit and vegetables. There seems to be far less that can go wrong, less dependence on a good summer or a late frost. So many of them will grow in tiny spaces, too: the balcony gardener who chooses carefully can end up with a greater crop of flavours than the gardener with half an acre at their disposal. This may look like a book about fripperies and finishing touches – there are indeed crystallised rose petals to drop into the bottom of your champagne glass and basil and mint sugar to scatter on your summer fruit – but it is also a book about layers of unexpected flavours; some punchy and hard to miss, some delicate and ethereal.

I want this, above all, to be a useful book. Each group of ingredients has its own growing information – which is the most finely flavoured rose to grow for petals? How do you grow tropical turmeric leaves when you garden in a distinctly non-tropical part of the world? – plus a little information about its uses in the kitchen. Next come the recipes: here are some ways in which I have enjoyed using these flavours myself. Finally, I have included cooking techniques that I have found particularly useful in drawing out and using these delicacies: warm infusions, pestos, seed butters and more. I hope these will act as a blueprint for further experimentation, inspiring you to play around with these lovely ingredients, finding your own combinations and ways. Taken all together this builds into a guide that will encourage gardeners to look at their gardens again, and tempt curious cooks to try out their green fingers. It will send you out into the garden primed to pluck the petal from the flower or the leaf from the plant that will turn the ordinary into something extraordinary.

# *Petal*

Primrose, forget-me-not, viola, lilac, borage, rose,
carnation, jasmine, pot marigold, nasturtium,
cornflower, daylily, garlic scape, artichoke, courgette
flower, pea flower, mustard flower, rosemary flower,
basil flower, lavender, chive flower, chamomile, thyme
flower, oregano flower, sage flower.

# Spring flowers

It just so happens that some of the first flowers of the year are edible: almost as soon as snows have thawed we can stroll out and start plucking pretty things for petal-strewn salads and flower-topped cakes. The selection of edible spring flowers are dominated by those that are simply edible rather than particularly appetising, and hence are used for their looks, but there are also a couple that have strong flavours to impart.

A little note that goes for all the flowers: if you grow them yourself to eat, never spray them with chemicals, and if you buy them in from specialist suppliers, make sure they have been grown organically. Also, whether from your garden or elsewhere, it is always a good idea to check for insects before you start cooking. Give whole flowers a good shake over a white plate, or if you are using petals then pull them off of the flower and drop them onto the plate, spreading them out to allow any little beasties to show themselves. You generally don't want to wash petals, as the flavours are so delicate, so this shaking and examining should be thorough.

### Primrose

These delicate, pale yellow flowers appear very early in the year, in fact the name – primrose – means first flower, or at least first rose. Most of the flower is close to flavourless but there is a small, sweet well at the base, the nectar that the bees are also after (so don't pick them all). Primrose is perennial and so will come back year after year, and slowly spread around the garden. It is a plant of dappled woodlands, so a spot under shrubs or trees or along the base of a hedge is perfect. Primroses look very pretty on spring salads alongside early hawthorn and sorrel leaves, but are just as good on sweets, either bare or crystallised.

### Forget-me-not

Nothing special at all in the flavour department, but forget-me-nots are worth a mention for their perfect, tiny, round petalled flowers, more like a graphic designer's imaginary flower than the real thing. Evenly spaced on the top of an iced cake they look particularly effective, but of course you can randomly sprinkle them, too, if that is more your style. Forget-me-nots are biennials – growing one year, the next flowering and then dying – and they will need sowing in early summer. They self-seed with great abandon so you should only ever need to do this once.

## Viola

The sweet violet, *Viola odorata*, rather spectacularly bucks the 'pretty but flavourless' trend followed by most of the spring flowers. Its flowers are strongly perfumed, the flavour they impart is floral and almost cloyingly sweet. Violets like the same woodland spot as the primulas and look beautiful side by side with them in the garden and the kitchen. They have traditionally been used to make a syrup. For every 1 cup of flowers – dry and with the green parts removed – pour over 1½ cups of boiling water and leave to steep for 24 hours. Squeeze out the flowers the next day and add 2 cups of sugar to every cup of water and heat gently. Never bring violet syrup to a full boil or it will lose its delicate colour, but heat to a gentle simmer, skim off any scum, then cool and bottle. Use in cocktails, over ice cream and in cakes and icing.

The rest of the violas and pansies are not scented or sweet and have more of a savoury, fresh, vegetable taste to them, however, they work well with both savoury and sweet dishes. Heartsease, *Viola tricolor*, is the best known. It has pretty little white, yellow and purple faces and has been cultivated for medicinal uses for centuries.

## Lilac

Lilac flowers smell better than they taste, but they are pretty and perfectly edible. If you want to try them, make a cold-water infusion – pour water over a bowlful of the flowers and leave it for an hour before straining it off and drinking it. The taste is subtle but pleasant enough. Better, though, to use these for decoration. Lilacs are easy-to-grow shrubs and are happy in most soils and situations. They are big and fairly dull for most of the year, but in my opinion they make up for it with their glamorous late-spring display and scent.

## Borage

One of the most familiar of all edible flowers is borage, often seen bobbing about on a sea of Pimm's, and with good reason. Borage tastes distinctly of cucumber, but not in an overly savoury way, so it is as happy on fruity desserts as it is on salads and gazpachos. It is a hardy annual and can be sown directly into the soil in autumn for spring flowering or in spring for summer flowering. Either way, you should only need to do this once as it is an enthusiastic self-seeder.

# Aviation with crystallised violets

The Aviation is a classic violet-based cocktail created in 1916 in New York. It is essentially a gin sour; a mix of sharp and sweet, with the sweet role being played by cherry and violet liqueurs. Violets love juicy red fruit so this makes for a fragrant, succulent and heady mix.

The name 'Aviation' refers to the vaguely unappetising sky-blue colour of the cocktail when you combine a clear maraschino liqueur with a violet one, but I prefer the juicier look you get when you use a deep red morello cherry liqueur – more of a stormy sky, perhaps, than a clear blue one. If you have made your own violet syrup (see page 10) it is a good substitute for the violet liqueur, which can be tricky to track down.

**Serves 1**

50ml gin

15ml morello cherry liqueur

7ml crème de violettes or violet syrup

20ml lemon juice

**To garnish**

1 crystallised violet

1 maraschino cherry

Pour all of the drink ingredients into a cocktail shaker and fill with ice. Shake and strain into a glass, then serve garnished with the crystallised violet and maraschino cherry.

# Blood oranges with lemon thyme cheesecake

This goat's cheese cake is dense and rich and needs some sharp fruit to accompany it. Later in the year you might make this again and use the blank canvas of the cheesecake topping for summer flowers and raspberries, but in spring there is a natural pairing of the last of the beautiful blood oranges with the first of the spring flowers. Blood orange, lemon thyme, almonds, honey and goat's cheese, the ingredients are so good that this is one of those desserts that feels like cheating.

**Serves 8**

**For the base**

450g almonds

4 tablespoons salted butter, melted

2 tablespoons honey

**For the topping**

300g soft rindless goat's cheese

100g cream cheese

50ml plain yogurt

2 tablespoons honey

1 teaspoon ground cinnamon

Small handful finely chopped lemon thyme, plus a few whole tips

Zest of 2 blood oranges, 1 pared, 1 finely grated

Spring flowers: primulas, forget-me-nots, lilacs

**For the oranges**

2 blood oranges, peeled and sliced thinly

1 tablespoon honey

1 teaspoon chopped lemon thyme

A few forget-me-not flowers

1. Preheat the oven to 180°C/gas mark 4. Line a spring-form or loose-bottomed cake tin with baking paper.

2. Put the almonds into a food-processor and pulse so that plenty of chunks remain, or pour them into a plastic bag and give them a good bash with a rolling pin until some are near dust and others are still chunky. In saucepan, warm the butter and honey then pour in the almonds, stirring until all are coated. Pour them into the base of the cake tin and press down evenly all over. Bake for 20 minutes, remove and leave to cool.

3. In a big bowl, combine the goat's cheese, cream cheese, yogurt, honey, cinnamon, finely chopped thyme and the grated orange zest (reserving the thyme tips and the pared zest). Mix and spread the topping out evenly on the cooled almond base. Place the tin in the fridge to set and chill for 1 hour or so.

4. When you are ready to serve, slide a knife between the baking paper and the tin and release the cheesecake. Gently pull away the paper from the base and use a knife to smooth and sharpen the edges. Decorate the top with the spring flowers, pared orange zest and thyme tips.

5. Lay the blood oranges on a plate so that you can see their stained glass-like qualities. Drizzle over the honey and sprinkle with the thyme and flowers. Serve alongside the cheesecake.

# Potted shrimp with fridge-pickled cucumber & borage

Borage, dill and cucumber are natural companions and come together with great ease. Both parts of this recipe are made ahead of time and are very transportable, so it makes a good picnic dish.

**Serves 2**

**For the pickle**

100ml white wine vinegar

100ml water

1 tablespoon salt (plus an extra 2 tablespoonfuls if you are salting the cucumbers, see tip below)

1 tablespoon caster sugar

½ teaspoon black peppercorns

½ cucumber, sliced into long ribbons using a mandoline or a vegetable peeler

1 tablespoon finely chopped dill, plus extra to serve

Borage flowers, to serve

**For the potted shrimp**

120g salted butter

Pinch of ground mace

Freshly grated nutmeg

Juice of ¼ lemon

200g peeled, cooked brown shrimps or prawns

Sea salt and freshly ground black pepper

1. To make the pickle, put the vinegar, water, salt, sugar and peppercorns into a saucepan and warm gently until the salt and sugar dissolve. Simmer for a minute and then remove from the heat to cool a little. Put the cucumber ribbons into a plastic container with a lid and sprinkle over the chopped dill. When the vinegar mixture is lukewarm, pour it over the cucumbers. Mix so that everything is coated, put the lid on and transfer to the fridge for 24 hours.

2. To make the potted shrimp, warm the butter gently in a small saucepan until the solids gather at the bottom. Gently pour off the clarified butter from the top, taking care to prevent the solids following. Discard the solids. Reserve a couple of tablespoonfuls of the clarified butter to finish the pots off and put the rest back into a clean saucepan and warm with the mace and nutmeg. Take off the heat and stir in the lemon juice and the salt and pepper. Divide the shrimps or prawns between two jars or ramekins and pour the butter over. Place in the fridge to set. When they are set, warm the reserved clarified butter and divide it between the two jars to seal them, and return the pots to the fridge to set again.

3. To serve the pickled cucumber, sprinkle on extra dill and top with the borage flowers. Remove the potted shrimps from the fridge and let them come back to room temperature before eating, served with brown bread.

*Tip*
*Fridge pickles are stored in the fridge and can be eaten the day after making, though they will keep for a few weeks. If you are not eating them immediately it is a good idea to salt the cucumber before pickling, which draws out excess liquid. Put a layer of the cucumber ribbons into a plastic container with a lid and sprinkle a little salt over them, then repeat until all of the layers are salted. Put the lid on and store in the fridge overnight. In the morning, wash off the salt and pat dry with kitchen paper, before proceeding with the pickling.*

15

# Pansy, beetroot & ewe's curd salad

These are violas in their savoury incarnation, looking pretty and purple among earthy beetroot, peppery rocket and tangy ewe's curd. If you can track down creamy, tangy ewe's curd, do – it is a gorgeous ingredient and perfect here – but if not, a soft, rindless goat's cheese will do the job.

**Serves 2**

3 beetroots, roasted until tender, cooled and skins removed

A couple of handfuls of rocket and baby rainbow chard leaves, washed and dried

150g ewe's curd or rindless goat's cheese log

A handful of violas and pansies

Cider vinegar

Extra virgin olive oil

Sea salt and freshly ground black pepper

Using a mandoline or sharp knife, slice the beetroots thinly and then arrange them on the plate with the salad leaves and generous spoonfuls of ewe's curd or goat's cheese. Scatter over the violas and pansies, then turn each face up. Sprinkle over a little vinegar, olive oil and salt and pepper, and serve.

# Crystallising

To crystallise is to coat a thing in sugar in order to preserve it and make it more delicious and beautiful, usually so it can be used as a garnish. Petals and whole flowers are beautiful crystallised, and even if a flower is perfectly edible and actually pretty tasty, coating it with sugar gives a very clear 'eat me' signal to the otherwise wary eater. Also try crystallising leaves, herb leaves in particular: a scattering of crystallised basil leaves on top of a strawberries-and-cream-filled sponge cake, or some crystallised mint leaves on your scoop of mint choc chip.

To crystallise flowers and leaves you will need: 1 egg white, ½ teaspoon high-proof vodka, caster sugar, a whisk, a fine paintbrush, tweezers, a tea strainer, a wire rack, baking paper, saint-like patience and plenty of time. Get all of your ingredients and equipment ready before you pick the flowers, if possible.

Whisk the egg white until it becomes a light foam and then add the vodka and whisk in. Holding the petal or flower at the base – with tweezers if necessary – paint it all over in the egg-white foam. Put a couple of teaspoons of sugar into the tea strainer and shake it over the flower, turning it as you do, until it is evenly coated. Place the baking paper onto the wire rack and the flower onto the baking paper. When you have finished crystallising, leave the rack in a cool and airy place (but not too airy, the flowers are feather-light), until the petals and flowers are dry and brittle. Store them between sheets of baking paper in an airtight container for up to two months.

# Summer flowers

Some of the most flavourful and commonly grown of edible blooms appear at the height of summer, during the long, warm and languid days when we are most likely to want to be strewing our food with something pretty and aromatic.

## Rose

Rose can turn dishes delicate and floral, a perfect English summer's day in pudding form, and in this guise it is beautiful in cakes or with strawberries and other summer fruits. It was used for centuries in English cooking before eventually falling out of favour as new hip flavourings replaced it; there are many old recipes such as tafferty tart (sliced apples with a rosewater icing) and rose wafers that were recorded in 'receipt' books of the 1700s.

While the English slowly fell out of love with rose, it has always been central to Middle Eastern and Indian cuisine. It is a crucial ingredient in the warm, pungent and sweet Moroccan spice mix, ras el hanout, which is used to flavour tagines, to sprinkle onto meat and is paired with orange blossom water, almonds and cinnamon to flavour sweet pastries and milky puddings with a subtle and dusky complexity. In Indian savoury cooking rosewater is often paired with almonds and saffron, as it is in some biryanis, particularly those made for celebrations such as Eid. It is teamed with cardamom and pistachios in *kheer*, an Indian rice pudding, and in *gulab jamun* it is made into a syrup with saffron and cardamom in which tiny donuts are drenched. It is when combined with these warming spices that it loses any sickly, soapy edge and becomes exotic.

Incorporate rose into dishes by using fresh petals, dried petals or rosewater (see page 36 for how to make distilled flower waters). I have read many times that you should snip away the pale base of the flower as it is bitter, but I have rarely done this and have noticed no difference in taste. The Middle East has traditionally been the centre of rosewater production, and is based mainly around one particular damask rose, 'Kazanlik', which is grown for its intensity of scent and oil. While 'Kazanlik' fares beautifully in Turkey and Iran, it does not grow particularly well in cooler climates. However, there are plenty of damasks that do, including 'Celsiana', 'Ispahan', 'La Ville de Bruxelles', 'Madame Hardy' and 'Marie Louise'. Gallica roses are also highly scented and perfect for edible use. Choose from *Rosa gallica* var. *officinalis*, 'Charles de Mills', 'Duchesse d'Angoulême', 'Duchesse de Montebello', 'Président de Sèze', 'Versicolor'/*Rosa mundi* and 'Tuscany Superb'. Plant in autumn or winter into rich, deep fertile soil or improve your soil prior to planting with plenty of organic matter, such as well-rotted farmyard manure.

### Carnations, clove pinks and gilly flowers

The petals of clove pinks have long been used in dishes for their sweet clove fragrance and taste. Once known as 'gilly flowers' ('July flowers') they often took the place of spices, where spices were too expensive to use. The best-flavoured are easily tracked down: they are the ones with the strongest scents.

Carnations and pinks both boast the Latin name *Dianthus*, but the split depends on which characteristics have been bred into them over the years. The term 'carnations' tends to mean those dianthus that need to be coddled under glass and that have sturdy, large flowers. Bred for looks and for cutting they have lost a good deal of their romance, along with their fragrance. Happily, for our purposes, pinks have a wonderful scent and flavour, and are also easy to grow. A little trivia: they are named after pinking shears because of the raggedy edge to their petals. The colour was named after the flowers.

'Sops-in-wine', one of the oldest varieties, was used to spice wine for weddings, and has red petals with a white blotch and a wonderful clove fragrance. 'Mrs Sinkins' is another old variety with a beautiful spiced scent and flavour, this time with white petals, and 'Inchmery' has a fresher, less heavily spicy scent and flavour and shell-pink flowers. Pinks are perennials and will produce flowers every summer over many years, but need a very well-drained soil and full sun.

### Jasmine

The pure white, star-shaped flowers of jasmine provide one of the best scents in the garden: powerful, sweet, spicy and abundant. It is with this aromatic perfume in mind that it should be used in cooking: dried to make a scented tea or infused in cream for delicate desserts. Jasmine also has savoury applications: a jasmine-infused vinegar or sauce is particularly lovely with seafood dishes.

Several plants get called variations on 'jasmine', so make sure you have the right one: *Jasminum officinale* and its cultivars (there is a lovely creamy flowered variety called 'Clotted Cream'). The others are all pretenders and a couple – Cape jasmine, *Gardenia jasminoides*, and Carolina jasmine, *Gelsemium sempervirens* – are poisonous. *Jasminum officinale* is a vigorous climbing plant and so needs a large and sturdy support in place before you plant it. Although it can grow well in sun or shade, it may not flower well (or at all) in shade.

### Pot marigold

The golden orange blooms of pot marigold are one of the most joyful and easily used of the edible flowers: throw a handful of the petals across just about any dish for instant sunshine. At home with both sweet and savoury dishes, they have traditionally been used for their colour above all else. Ground up they make a good alternative to saffron or turmeric, turning sauces and butters golden-hued. They do have a subtly peppery flavour, though it is not strong. Grind petals in oil to make a glistening golden salad oil, or dry them and add to stews for rich colouring. Mostly I scatter them over salads and fruit salads.

You will want to find seeds or plants of pot marigold, *Calendula officinalis*, not to be confused with African or French marigolds, which are not edible. Sow in early autumn or spring. Straight *Calendula officinalis* is hi-vis-vest orange, but I also plant *C.o.* 'Indian Prince', which has darker orange petals with dark red backs, and *C.o.* 'Art Shades', which is various shades of orange and apricot.

## Nasturtium

Nasturtium flowers are peppery, sweet and crisp. The colours of the flowers are dazzling in reds, oranges and yellows, and they look stunning topping salads. They are annuals but great self-seeders, so you shouldn't have to sow them more than once unless you want a particular shade. They are sensitive to frost, so your first sowing should be in spring indoors. I like the dark red 'Mahogany Jewel', but also wouldn't be without the jumble of colours that you get from a mix such as 'Whirlybird Mixed'. Paler-coloured flowers tend to be gentler in flavour in my experience. A quick word about the leaves of nasturtium: they are edible and have a peppery flavour. I like to use the usual green ones as a salad leaf, mixed in with the dramatically white- and pale-green-splashed leaves of 'Alaska'.

## Cornflower

Though its flavour is nothing to write home about, cornflower is perfectly edible and useful for adding a splash of gorgeous sapphire blue. Being fairly tasteless, you can sprinkle it whenever you want brighten up a dish. A hardy annual, it needs to be sown in autumn or spring each year. Autumn sowings will produce bigger, stronger plants that will flower earlier. *Centaurea cyanus* 'Blue Boy' is the cultivar to choose for the best blue, and 'Black Ball' is a good dark purple.

23

## Daylily

In the eating, daylilies have most in common with the vegetable flowers. They are large, crunchy and sweetly vegetal, and yet they very much sit in the flower border and not in the vegetable patch. They have most in common with courgette flowers, and can be used in very similar ways: stuffed and baked or deep fried, fried in butter or shredded and scattered raw on salads.

They are very good-looking plants, perennial in habit and producing large, lily-like flowers all through the summer, even in shade. The name daylily comes from the fact that each flower lasts just one day, fading and turning limp as dusk falls. This is in the favour of those who want to eat them, as they are still delicious when faded, and harvesting has precisely no impact on the overall display. The darker red-flowered varieties can have a hint of bitterness, so go for paler ones such as yellow *Hemerocallis lilioasphodelus*, or *H.* 'White Temptation'. Plants are not particularly fussy about soil or amount of sunlight, but ideally plant them in spring and keep watered over their first summer. They will die down over winter each year but leap back into life come spring, slowly clumping up over time.

# Ras el hanout & sour cherry meatballs

This is one of my favourite ways of using ras el hanout, the warm and sweet spice mix that contains dried rose petals. Put a sprinkle on top of the dish, too, for a finishing touch.

**Serves 4, with rice or pitta breads**

**For the tomato sauce**

1 onion, diced

Vegetable oil, for frying

400g can tomatoes

1 cinnamon stick

Splash of red wine vinegar

Sea salt and freshly ground black pepper

**For the meatballs**

400g minced lamb

1 egg

2 tablespoons ras el hanout

1 onion, grated

100g dried sour cherries, chopped

**For the tahini sauce**

2 tablespoons tahini

4 tablespoons yogurt

Juice of ½ lemon

**To finish**

Chopped mint

Dried rose petals

Ras el hanout

1. On a low–medium heat, sauté the onion in a frying pan or saucepan with a little oil until they start to turn translucent. Add the tomatoes, cinnamon, a splash of red wine vinegar and seasoning and bring to a gentle simmer. Cook slowly, stirring occasionally, until the sauce thickens a little.

2. Put all of the meatball ingredients into a large bowl, season with salt and pepper and mix with your hands, massaging everything together for several minutes to tenderise the meat. Form into little golf-ball-sized balls (or smaller if you like – kids seem to particularly like tiny ones) and then fry them in a pan with a little oil over a high heat for several minutes on each side until browned. Tip them into the tomato sauce and simmer gently for 30 minutes.

3. To make the tahini sauce, mix the tahini, yogurt, lemon juice and a little salt and pepper in a bowl. Take the meatballs in the sauce to the table, top with the tahini sauce and a scattering of mint, rose petals and ras el hanout.

# Rosie fruit salad with rose, rosé & strawberry sorbet

This is rose at its pinkest and most joyfully summery. The sorbet is boozy, fruity and floral and it looks pretty with a jumble of pink and purple summer fruits.

**Serves 4**

**For the sorbet**

500ml rosé wine

130g sugar

350g strawberries

1–2 teaspoons rosewater

A small handful of rose petals, torn up

**For the fruit salad**

200g strawberries, hulled and halved

200g raspberries

150g cherries, halved and stoned

¼ watermelon, seeds discarded, flesh cut into cubes

4 figs, quartered

1. To make the sorbet, combine the wine and the sugar in a saucepan and heat and stir until the sugar has dissolved. Bring briefly to the boil and then remove from the heat and drop the strawberries into the pan. Leave the mixture to cool and then use a hand-held electric blender to purée it. Chill in the fridge until cold. (It helps to wait until the mixture is cold before you purée the fruit as cold dampens the flavours.)

2. Once cold, add the rosewater, one teaspoon at a time, tasting as you go. You want to make sure the rose can be tasted, but avoid an overly floral and soapy flavour. When you are happy with your rosiness, churn the chilled mixture in an ice-cream maker, dropping in the handful of rose petals towards the end of the churn. Pour into a freezerproof container, cover with a lid and freeze. The sorbet will not get particularly stiff in the ice-cream maker but do not fear as it will freeze to the perfect scoopable consistency after 30 minutes or so in the freezer.

3. To make the fruit salad, combine all of the fruits in a bowl. Remove the sorbet from the freezer and scoop out two portions. Either serve immediately or set them aside to melt and pour over the fruits, stirring to combine.

# Jasmine tea ice cream with lychees & jasmine flowers

Jasmine tea contains dried jasmine flowers and green tea, making for a subtly sweet and highly fragrant drink. Infused in milk this tea makes the base for a grown-up and complex ice cream, perfect for pairing with delicate and fragrant lychees. Have a couple of jasmine blooms to hand for extra fragrance, or you could crystallise them (see page 18) and eat them, too.

**Serves 6–8**

500ml full-fat milk

2 tablespoons jasmine tea

125g caster sugar

6 egg yolks

150ml double cream

A few lychees per serving

1. Put the milk into a saucepan and bring it just to the boil. Remove from the heat and add the jasmine tea. Leave to infuse for 10 minutes. Whisk together the sugar and the egg yolks in a large bowl and then strain on the milky tea infusion, whisking all the time. Clean out the pan, pour the mixture into it and set it onto a low heat. It is a good idea to have a basin full of cold water in the sink as you do this, and a clean whisk to hand, as they will help you rescue the mix should it start curdling. Stir the mixture continually with a wooden spoon over the low heat. After about 10 minutes it should start to thicken, and it is ready as soon as you can draw a clear line through the custard that coats the back of the spoon.

2. Once the custard is made, set it aside to cool (you can speed this up by placing the pan in the basin of cold water and stirring, curdled or not). Once cool, chill completely in the fridge.

3. Just before churning the cold custard in the ice-cream maker, whisk the double cream in a large bowl to soft peaks and mix it into the custard. Churn the ice-cream mixture and then transfer to a freezerproof container with a lid and put in the freezer until it is frozen, about 6 hours or overnight.

4. Remove the ice cream from the freezer 20 minutes before you want to eat it, to let it soften, before serving it with the lychees.

*Tip*
*A note about curdling, as it happens so often it is best to be prepared: As you cook the custard watch it closely and at the first signs of a bitty texture developing remove the pan from the heat and plunge the base of the pan into cold water, whisking vigorously, and making sure none of the water spills over into the pan. Keep whisking until the mixture looks smooth.*

# Braised rainbow veg with nasturtium flower labneh

Labneh is essentially yogurt with flavours added and then strained until it takes on a soft-cheese consistency. It is very simple to make but does need to be started the day before you are going to eat it. It is a good vehicle for peppery and colourful nasturtium flowers and is delicious with glorious, tender and sweet early summer vegetables, which really shine after a short braise in a buttery, flavour-filled stock.

**Serves 4**

**For the labneh**

500g plain yogurt

About 12 nasturtium flowers, torn into pieces

Sea salt and freshly ground black pepper

**For the braised vegetables**

100ml white wine

100ml water

50g salted butter

Juice of ½ lemon

1 teaspoon fennel seeds

1 bay leaf

4 garlic cloves, peeled

12 shallots, peeled and halved

12 baby carrots, scrubbed and trimmed

12 radishes, halved

12 asparagus spears, tough ends trimmed off

12 mangetout pods

1. To make the labneh, mix the yogurt, petals, salt and pepper in a bowl. Take a cheesecloth and drape it over a colander, then spoon the yogurt mixture into the centre. Lift the corners of the cheesecloth so that all of the yogurt falls into the centre of the cloth and find somewhere that this can hang and drip. (I hang mine from an overhead kitchen cupboard handle, with a bowl sitting on the worktop below it.) Leave it to strain for around 24 hours.

2. The next day, put the wine, water, butter, lemon juice, fennel seeds, bay leaf and garlic into a wide pan over a medium heat. Bring to a gentle simmer for a few minutes and then add the shallots. Simmer for about 5 minutes until they start to soften and then add the carrots and simmer for another few minutes. Add the radishes, asparagus spears and mangetout pods for the last few minutes of cooking. Remove the vegetables from the pan using a slotted spoon or tongs and moisten them with a little of the cooking liquor. Serve with the turned-out labneh and some good bread.

# Petal cake

This is a lovely enough cake – a basic lemony sponge brightened with a flowery confetti – but above all it is an excuse to create beautiful concentric rings of petals: a spectacle for a special occasion. You need patience, cups of tea, a burbling radio and plenty of time to complete the petal topping satisfactorily, but if you have such things then there are few lovelier ways to spend a morning.

**Serves 8**

**For the cake**

200g salted butter

200g caster sugar

Zest of 1 lemon

1 teaspoon vanilla essence

4 eggs

200g self-raising flour

1 teaspoon baking powder

Cornflower and marigold petals, about a mug full

**For the butter icing and petal topping**

150g salted butter

275g golden icing sugar

Grated zest and juice of 1 lemon

Cornflower and marigold petals

1. Preheat the oven to 180°C/gas mark 4 and line two 23cm cake tins with baking parchment.

2. In a large bowl, cream the butter, sugar, lemon zest and vanilla essence together with a hand-held electric mixer until fluffy. Then add the eggs, one at a time, mixing until each is thoroughly combined before adding the next. Sift the flour and baking powder into the bowl and fold in until well combined. Add the petals to the mixture and stir in. Divide the mixture between the two cake tins and smooth the tops, then bake for around 35 minutes, or until they are risen and golden and a cocktail stick poked into the centre comes out clean. Leave to cool in the tins for 10 minutes then turn out and cool completely on a wire rack.

3. When the cakes are cool, make the icing by beating the butter with a hand-held electric mixer until it is soft and fluffy and adding a little icing sugar at a time, beating until it is completely combined before adding more. To finish, add the lemon zest and a little lemon juice to loosen the mix (beat well to prevent curdling). Spread a third of the icing over the top of one cake, position the second cake on top and spread another third of the icing on top of that. Use the final third of the icing to cover the sides of the cake.

4. You will need to be ready to decorate with the petals straight away as the icing hardens slightly over time, which prevents them sticking easily (though you can moisten the top with a little water from a mister or a pastry brush if this happens). Starting on the outside of the cake, create rings of concentric petals of contrasting colours, continuing until you reach the middle. Eat the cake the same day, as the petals quickly lose their freshness.

# Sops in wine, or clove pinks in prosecco jelly

The petals of clove pinks were once used to spice and flavour wines, particularly for celebrations such as weddings, and I thought it would be pretty and fun to make a celebration jelly based on this idea. The trick to capturing the prosecco bubbles in the jelly is to work quickly and to have everything as cold as possible before you start.

**Serves 6**

100g pineberries or alpine strawberries, halved

150g blueberries

50ml honey

Petals from 10 fragrant clove pinks

8 sheets of gelatine

750ml prosecco, thoroughly chilled

1. Take six wine glasses or small glass bowls and divide the fruits between them, then chill in the fridge for at least 30 minutes.

2. Warm the honey just a little in a small saucepan and drop in half of the petals. Remove from the heat, stir them in and leave them to infuse.

3. Put the gelatine sheets into a bowl of cold water and leave to soak for 10 minutes. When it has softened, first remove the petals from the honey and discard, then lift the gelatine sheets from the water, squeeze out any excess water and drop them into the warm honey. They should start to dissolve, but if they don't, warm the honey slightly until they do.

4. Open the prosecco and immediately pour it, a little at a time, into the honey mixture, working fairly quickly and stirring all the time. Remove the glasses or bowls from the fridge, divide the mixture between them, scatter with the remaining petals, and return to the fridge immediately. Leave to set overnight, or for at least 6 hours.

# Distilled flower waters

You can make your own rosewater for flavouring creams, yogurts, cakes and more. By doing so you can be sure that your petals have not been sprayed with any chemicals, but the technique also allows you to make more unusual distilled waters with a variety of scented flowers: violet, carnation, lavender and jasmine waters are all useful for adding aromatic flavours to sweet dishes. Pick around a dozen roses that have just opened (or a few cupfuls of the other flowers) – ideally first thing in the morning, when their flavour is at its most potent. Pull their petals off and put them into a saucepan, taking care not to include any green parts. A saucepan with a glass lid is ideal.

Pour about 1 litre of water over the petals (or enough water to fill the saucepan about half way). Float a small bowl on the surface and then put the saucepan lid on upside down. Bring to the boil and simmer gently. As soon as the water begins to condense on the underside of the upturned lid, place a few ice cubes onto it, as this will encourage more condensation at the centre. You will have to soak up the melted ice cubes occasionally with kitchen paper or a tea towel (and do make sure your saucepan lid has no holes in it through which the melted ice water can drip). After about an hour you will have a bowl full of flower-flavoured liquid. Lift it out and let it cool, then transfer to a sterilised bottle and store in the refrigerator until needed.

# Vegetable flowers

Vegetable flowers are not eaten for wafts of aromatics or haunting hints. No, they are solid and crunchy and some could make a decent meal all by themselves. They taste of the vegetable from which they came, but milder, and sweeter. Their appearance is a fleeting moment on the plant's journey towards proper vegetable production, and therefore is all the more precious and seasonal.

### Garlic scapes

These are the flowers of garlic, but not just any old garlic; scapes are only thrown up by the hardneck garlics – known as the gourmet garlics because of their more interesting flavours. Their scapes appear very briefly in early summer, a little treat of a pre-harvest, and you do the plant a favour by picking them as they sap energy from the swelling bulb. They are delicious: sweetly and mildly garlicky with a vegetable-like crunch. Steam them, roast them, barbecue them or blend them up into pesto. Just be sure to enjoy them for their few brief weeks.

### Artichoke

We grow artichokes for their flowers, or at least for their flower buds, as they become utterly inedible by the time the flowers open. Choose a spot in well-drained soil and full sun and they will normally start producing heads in their second year. Plants are at their most productive aged 3–5 years, after which the yield starts to decline.

Harvest the flower buds well before they open, when the outer petals are still curving inwards. Cut them with a few centimetres of stem and then drop the entire stem into a pan of boiling salted water, weighing the flower down with a small lid to keep it underwater. Boil until the whole head has become softened and an outer petal pulls away very easily, then drain and serve, pulling away the petals one by one and eating them dipped into hollandaise or mayonnaise. When you reach it, remove the inedible hairy choke, then eat on to the heart below.

### Courgette

Where once I planted in order to harvest courgettes, I realise my gardening has slowly evolved to the point where I plant as much for courgette flowers as for their fruits. If you want courgettes, my advice is never to plant more than three plants, any more and you will have a massive glut and be handing out carrier-bagfuls – along with a jar of courgette jam and one or two bottles of courgette ketchup. If you are planting for flowers you need to break this rule and plant lots: I grow at least ten plants these days.

You need to pick the flowers before they turn into fruits, or pick them with little tender fruits still attached. I promise you will never get sick of them, and nor will your neighbours. Sometimes the plants will produce male flowers, which will never turn into courgettes anyway, and these you can pick with abandon without harming any potential courgette crop. You can tell the difference by looking at the back of the flowers: female flowers have the small beginnings of a fruit attached, male flowers just meet the stem directly. Some varieties are supposed to produce more male than female flowers and therefore are particularly good for flower production, 'Bianca' being one such. I generally plant a few of these and then one or two each of several other varieties, so that the miniature courgettes attached to my courgette flowers are all different shapes and colours. Pleasing. They are tender annuals so you will need to start them from seed in spring and only plant them out once all danger of frost has passed.

Courgette flowers are delicate and delicious and can be cooked in all sorts of ways, not just battered and deep fried, which – though very good indeed – can mask the delicate vegetable taste. I love them just fried in butter until crispy and then finished off with a little lemon juice and sea salt, but they are also marvellous stuffed and baked, or just shredded and eaten raw on top of a salad.

### Pea and mangetout flowers

Every part of the pea plant is edible and every part of it tastes of pea. The flowers are good additions to salads or to top any dishes that would benefit from this fresh taste. Pea flowers are generally white, and nice enough, but mangetout flowers are bicoloured pink and purple, and make more of a splash.

Pea and mangetout plants are pretty hardy and can take some frost, although they will struggle in really cold soil. Sow early in the year indoors and plant out as the weather warms and growth starts to pick up. You will need to provide some supports for your plants to clamber up. Protect the young shoots from slugs and cover them with mesh to prevent birds eating them while they are getting started. Pick the flowers while they are young and fresh; they are produced in such abundance that you still get plenty of peas or mange tout as well.

### Mustard flowers

The oriental mustards such as komatsuna, mizuna, mibuna and tatsoi are grown for their spicy and peppery leaves, providing welcome green leafiness over the colder months. As the plants reach the end of their productive lives they will often go to flower. Most people pull them up and throw them onto the compost heap at this point, but hold on: the flowers are small, pretty and bright yellow, and have much of the pungency of the leaves. They are unapologetically savoury. Use them wherever something hot and peppery would be welcome: on mild and creamy potato salads, with smoked mackerel or on a seared beef salad.

# *Carciofi alla giudia:* Jewish-style artichokes

This style of serving artichokes hails from Rome's Jewish quarter. To my mind it is the most flowery looking of all methods of artichoke preparation, which is one of the reasons I wanted to include it here. It is also a truly gorgeous coming-together of soft and tender innards and perfectly crisp outer layers, which is perhaps a better reason.

**Serves 2, as a starter**

4 artichoke heads

Vegetable or sunflower oil, for frying

1 lemon, cut into wedges

Sea salt

1. Pull off all of the tough green outer petals of the artichoke heads until only the paler, softer ones are left. Slice off the stubs of these petals using a sharp paring knife and then peel the stem using a y-peeler. Make the stem no more than a few centimetres long. Start to remove the top two thirds or so of each individual petal, removing all spikes and leaving only soft, tender yellow bases. Once you have attended to each of the petals around the sides, cut the central point of the petals. The aim throughout should not be to cut straight across the artichoke head, and you should end up with something that most resembles a fully double rose or a ranunculus flower, slightly domed and with many curved petals. If you are using baby artichokes you can stop there, but on larger artichokes use a teaspoon to scoop out the hairy choke at the centre. Normally you would need to pop these into acidified water after cutting to prevent them from going brown, but as they are going to be deep fried anyway there is no need.

2. Prepare a basin or bowl of iced water and then bring a large saucepan full of salted water to the boil. Cook the artichokes in the pan for a few minutes, until they are tender and easily pierced with a skewer. Remove them from the boiling water using a slotted spoon and plunge them straight into the iced water. When they are cool, remove them and lay them out on layers of kitchen paper, face down, having spread the petal stubs out first. Leave them to drain and dry for 30 minutes or so.

3. Heat a saucepan full of oil to 160°C (or test it is ready by throwing in a small breadcrumb, if it sizzles immediately it is ready). Cook the artichokes for a couple of minutes, turning them occasionally, until they are crispy and brown. Remove and drain on dry kitchen paper. Serve immediately, with the lemon wedges and a sprinkling of sea salt crystals.

# Charred garlic scapes with romesco sauce

This is a garlicky take on the Spanish tradition of the calcotada, in which young spring onions (calcots) are charred and served with romesco sauce for dipping.

**Serves 2**

30 garlic scapes

Olive oil

Sea salt and freshly ground black pepper

**For the romesco sauce**

2 red peppers

1 onion, diced

Olive oil, for frying

1 large tomato, peeled, deseeded and chopped

1 teaspoon smoked paprika

50g blanched almonds, roasted

50g blanched hazelnuts, roasted

1 garlic clove

1 slice of good white bread, cut into chunks

Splash of extra virgin olive oil

Splash of red wine vinegar

1. First make the sauce. Put your red peppers under a hot grill and blacken them thoroughly on all sides. Place them into a large bowl and cover this tightly with clingfilm, then leave them to cool. (The steam this creates will help to separate the skin from the flesh.) When they are completely cool, peel away the blackened skins, roughly chop the flesh and set aside.

2. Meanwhile, fry the onion in a little olive oil until it is soft, then add the tomato, paprika and a little water and cook to a jammy consistency. Put the nuts and the garlic into a food-processor and whizz them to coarse sandy texture (or you could do this, more laboriously, in a pestle and mortar). Add the bread along with the tomato mixture, the peppers, a little extra virgin olive oil and a splash of red wine vinegar. Pulse to combine all, but leave the sauce chunky and textured.

3. Heat a barbecue until the coals are white. Put the garlic scapes into a large bowl and pour on a little olive oil, then mix to coat all of the scapes. Cook on the barbecue for a few minutes on each side, then serve with the romesco, a slice of good bread and a glass of red wine.

# Wrapping & stuffing

Some leaves and flowers from the garden are at their best when wrapped around other foods, either acting as an edible casing to be chomped through, or as a flavoured steamer, infusing the foods within with their own inimitable tastes.

Top of the heap in the first category are courgette flowers, which are delicious in themselves and have a sweet, delicate courgette flavour. Good enough raw, they are most beloved when stuffed and cooked. To prepare courgette flowers for eating you need to remove the stigma or stamen – the inner parts of the flower. Gently ease the petals open, slip two fingers into the opening and grab the parts, tugging at or bending them to snap them off. Remove and discard, then stuff the petals with whatever filling you like – ricotta, leftover risotto and mince are all good. You will need a teaspoon and a delicate touch to do this. Dip the stuffed flowers into a basic batter (whisk an egg yolk and 15ml ice cold water into 125g plain flour and a pinch of salt) and deep-fry them, or bed them down on a rich tomato sauce, smother in cheese and bake.

Banana leaves have long been used in the cuisines of the Far East and India as the ultimate living steamer. They are best suited to savoury dishes and impart a grassy, vegetable taste to whatever is cooked within: fish, chicken, rice and all. You can trap aromatic herbs inside a pouch created by folding a leaf over on itself and pinning the two sides of the leaf together with cocktail sticks. I have also used two lengths of the leaf ribs for wrapping: marinade some pieces of chicken then lay them along one length of rib, cover with the other, and seal shut at either end with cocktail sticks. Either method produces a package ready for baking, steaming or placing direct onto the barbecue.

Turmeric leaves are the sweet alternative: use them to wrap coconut and jiggery dumplings known as patholi, or to wrap bananas and pineapple for barbecuing or steaming. The turmeric leaves impart a sweet, gently spicy and citrusy flavour.

There are other flavoured leaves that can be used in similar ways. Wrap fig leaves around cheese, fish or fruit and they will be impregnated with the leaves' coconutty flavour as they cook. Also try fig leaves pushed into muffin trays to act as cake cases or to line a loaf tin and they will act as both baking parchment and perfumer: for example, try a fig-leaf-baked yogurt and honey cake topped with a piece of fig.

# Stuffed & baked courgette flowers with soured cream, preserved lemon & mint dressing

The first courgette flowers always arrive on my plot at the same time as the first broad beans and early peas, so that is what I like to bake them with. I use fresh broad beans because I have them to hand but there is no harm in using frozen ones.

**Serves 2, as a starter**

500g shelled broad beans (about 2kg in their shells)

150g cream cheese

50g Parmesan cheese, finely grated

Sea salt and freshly ground black pepper

10 courgette flowers

Extra virgin olive oil, for drizzling

75g pine nuts, toasted

**For the dressing**

150ml soured cream

1 tablespoon extra virgin olive oil

1 preserved lemon, deseeded and finely chopped

2 tablespoons finely chopped mint

1. Preheat your oven to 190°C/gas mark 5.

2. Drop the beans into a large pan of boiling salted water and cook for 1 minute. Drain, and tip into a bowl of iced water. Drain into a colander and double-pod them, removing the pale green and bitter outer casing, then put them into a large bowl and add the cream cheese, Parmesan and a good pinch each of salt and pepper. Mash with a fork or use a hand-held electric blender, but make sure you leave plenty of beans intact, for a bit of texture.

3. Prepare the courgette flowers ready for stuffing (see page 44 – wrapping and stuffing) then use a teaspoon to fill the cavity with the broad bean mixture; a couple of teaspoons is most probably the most you will need, dependent on the size of the flower. Twist the tips of the petals together around the stuffing to seal. When all have been filled, scatter any leftover stuffing into a baking dish and nestle the courgette flowers into it. Pour on a little extra virgin olive oil and sprinkle with salt and pepper, then bake for 15 minutes in the oven.

4. To make the dressing, mix together the soured cream, extra virgin olive oil, preserved lemon, mint and a little salt and pepper to taste.

5. The baked courgette flowers are best served warm but not piping hot; just before taking them to the table, pour on the dressing and sprinkle with the pine nuts.

# Seared hot & sour beef salad with mustard flowers

Beef and mustard are fine companions and a handful of bright yellow and piquant mustard flowers work well with this classic warm salad – even more so if you can track down baby oriental mustard leaves.

**Serves 2**

250g beef fillet steak

**For the dressing**

2 tablespoons fish sauce

2 tablespoons lime juice

1 teaspoon caster sugar

1 red chilli, deseeded and finely chopped

**For the salad**

130g baby oriental mustard leaves (or other baby salad leaves)

1 spring onion, finely sliced

1 large carrot, peeled and cut into batons

½ cucumber, cut into batons

A handful of coriander leaves, roughly chopped

100g peanuts, roasted, salted and crushed

A handful of mustard flowers

1. Make the dressing by combining the fish sauce, lime juice, sugar and chilli in a bowl.

2. On a large serving platter, lay out the baby oriental mustard leaves, spring onion, carrot and cucumber.

3. In a medium-hot frying pan, sear the beef for around 3 minutes on each side. Remove from the pan to a plate and leave to rest for a few minutes.

4. Move the beef to a chopping board and slice into fine strips, then put all of the strips into the dressing and mix well to coat.

5. Arrange the beef over the leaves and then pour over the remainder of the dressing so that everything is at least slightly coated. Top with the coriander leaves, crushed peanuts and mustard flowers and serve warm.

47

# Scallops, chorizo & pea flowers

This is just a lovely meeting of ingredients that get along very well; a quick and easy way to celebrate the pea harvest and the moment that mangetout flowers and pods are at their freshest and pretty best.

**Serves 2**

10 slices of chorizo

150g podded peas (frozen is fine)

6 scallops

12 mangetout pods

12 mangetout or pea shoots

12 mangetout or pea flowers

1 lemon wedge

1. Fry the chorizo in a medium-hot frying pan until the edges are crisp and plenty of the deep orange oil has escaped. Remove them from the pan and arrange them straight onto serving plates, leaving the oil in the pan. Put the peas in the pan, cooking (or defrosting) them for a few minutes and lightly crushing a few with a fork or spatula, then lift them out and arrange them on the plates with the chorizo. With the pan hot, sear the scallops for a few minutes on each side, until they are nicely browned, and add them to the plates.

2. Arrange the mangetout pods, and mangetout or pea shoots and flowers on the plates and pour over the remnants of the oil, squeeze over some lemon juice and serve.

# Herb flowers

The flowers of herbs are a subtler and much more beautiful way of incorporating herb flavours into your food. All are more delicate in taste than their leaves, but still strong enough to make their presence felt.

### Rosemary

The wonderful thing about rosemary is its timing: the flowers appear early in the year, when little else is in flower, pleasing both cooks and bees. I like to use them in sweet recipes, but they are also good in savoury breads, where the taste is gentler than that of the more resinous leaf. Anywhere you would normally infuse rosemary and then remove it, you can throw in handfuls of their flowers with impunity. A native of Mediterranean scrubland, it is at its happiest planted in well-drained soil in full sun when its leaves and flowers will contain the highest amount of pungent, aromatic oils. It is also a survivor, and is worth trying even if you cannot give it such idyllic conditions. Like all of the silver-leaved Mediterranean herbs, rosemary is relatively short-lived, so be prepared to replace it when it gets leggy and woody. Silver-leaved plants hate to be cut back hard into old wood, so trim it back lightly every year after flowering instead.

### Basil

Like the leaves, basil flowers marry well with Mediterranean vegetables but also have an affinity with fruits such as strawberries, raspberries and peaches. Mediterranean strains descended from sweet basil, *Ocimum basilicum,* have pure white, fairly insignificant, flowers. The purple spires on dark stems of oriental basils are far more impressive, with stronger hints of liquorice, cloves and cinnamon. A whole flower head or two of *Ocimum* × *africanum* 'Siam Queen' or holy basil, *O. tenuiflorum,* as the final ingredient in a pho or other clear soup will be both beautiful and highly aromatic.

An annual, basil needs to be sown afresh every year. It's a heat lover, and sulks or just plain dies in the variable temperatures of a typical spring. If you are growing a straightforward variety it is sensible to buy plants, but if you want to grow lots or one of the more unusual forms you will have to sow seeds. Start these off in a heated propagator, then keep the seedlings warm and in a bright place. What they dislike most is a big temperature difference between night and day, so keep in a consistently warm spot until the weather is reliably warm outside. They love to grow in a polytunnel or greenhouse all summer long. Once they are in full growth, water and feed them well. Flowers will appear towards late summer.

## Lavender

Strident: sweet, strong and unmissable in whatever food it touches, lavender contains hints of mint, rosemary and camphor, but can easily tip over into unpleasantly soapy and floral if used too generously. It has an affinity for dairy, so infuse it in custards, hot chocolates and ice creams. It also enhances fruit beautifully, notably strawberries and cherries, and has an often overlooked savoury side. It is sometimes included in 'herbes de Provence' and alongside dried rose petals in ras el hanout. Try making a lavender salt using dried heads mixed with sea salt flakes, for use on seafood, or sprinkle the broken heads over savoury dairy, such as goat's cheese, before baking. It is also subtle and sweet cooked with lamb; its herbal, astringent qualities cutting through the fattiness of the meat.

Like rosemary, lavender is a Mediterranean silver-leaved shrub, and it should be grown in much the same way. The so-called English varieties, such as *Lavandula angustifolia*, are best for cooking, being lower in the less-pleasant camphor notes. Lavender flowers are at their best when the petals are just showing a flash of colour. To store, pick them on a dry day with long stalks attached and hang upside down in bunches in a dark, airy spot until completely dry. Store in an airtight jar with a little rice to absorb moisture. The flower buds can also be used fresh.

## Chive

Chive flowers appear in late spring. Unambiguously savoury, they belong to the allium family, but the flavour is subtly oniony with a hint of garlic, and not at all overpowering. Chives do not need full sun to grow, and in fact are one of the few herbs that can thrive in shade. However, you will get more flowers if your plant sees a little sunlight every now and then. A perennial, chives need only be planted once, but will die down over winter, to emerge fresh and soft the following spring. Look out for white-flowered types if you like something different, but they all taste much the same.

## Chamomile

Chamomile flowers have an interesting aroma and taste: apple and honey but musky and earthy too. But it isn't a flavour that everyone gets along with (Peter Rabbit endured chamomile tea as a punishment for losing his new jacket) and it can sometimes be bitter. Its most common use is as a tisane and it's a particularly good one at bedtime, being calming and slumber-inducing, but it can also be used in honey and chamomile ice cream, in a syrup, or with summer fruits. *Chamaemelum nobile*, the type used for scented chamomile lawns, is not the sort we are after. German chamomile, *Matricaria chamomilla,* is an annual and grows taller, and this is the one that produces honey-apple-scented flowers. Sow the seeds on the surface of a pot of seed compost indoors in early spring. Pot them on as they grow and plant out when the weather has warmed. They are enthusiastic self-seeders, so with a bit of luck you should only have to do this once. The flowers appear throughout summer; harvest them when they are fully open by running your fingers up between a group of stems and pulling lightly.

## Thyme

A member of the mint family, thyme has hints of mint about it, but with a mellower, more complex, faintly resinous flavour. Despite its savoury notes, I love it in creamy desserts, and with fruit, where it offers an unexpected counterbalance. The flowers appear in summer and have a gentler, sweeter taste than the leaves. Use both thyme stalks and flowers in breads, in anything that contains lemon (they are natural friends), with chicken, seafood and cheese. The difference between the two is in delicacy: the leaves can be slow-cooked in stews and roasts; the flowers should be a last-minute addition. An evergreen, thyme grows as a little subshrub or creeping plant. Grow in full sun in well-drained soil and harvest the leaves and flowers throughout summer, trimming the plant all over in mid-to-late summer to encourage bushiness. Common thyme, *Thymus vulgaris*, and its varieties are the most commonly used for cooking. Lemon thyme, *T. citriodorus,* has a strong lemon fragrance and taste, *T.* 'Fragrantissimus' has more of an orange flavour, and T. *herba-barona* is known as caraway thyme for its strong caraway fragrance and taste.

## Oregano

To my taste, oregano is similar to thyme, only with a wilder, more pungent flavour. Grown in a similar way, as a small subshrub, in sun and well-drained soil, it's kept bushy by nipping out the shoots and the flowers. The leaves are good in tomato sauces and scattered onto the feta cheese on the top of a Greek salad, as are the flowers, if treated delicately. *Origanum vulgare,* common oregano, is the one most often used for cooking. Greek oregano, *O. v.* subsp. *hirtum* 'Greek', is stronger, although unfortunately plants won't obtain that full wild Greek mountain flavour when grown in cooler, damper climates.

## Sage

Sage flowers are produced in impressive purple spires in early summer and have the same musky, savoury flavour as the leaves. Used on salads and pasta, they add complexity of flavour and a dash of colour. Despite their obvious leaning to the savoury they can venture into sweet territory, rubbing up well with apples in particular. Another silver-leaved Mediterranean shrub, it should be grown much like the others, in full sun and well-drained soil, with a light trim after flowering. *Salvia officinalis*, the common grey-leaved sage, is perfect for cooking and for producing flowers, but *S. o.* 'Tricolor' has pretty white and grey-green variegated foliage flushed with purple, while *S. o.* 'Purpurascens' has purple-grey leaves. They all taste the same, though, and all produce flowers.

# Tomato salad with sage flowers & basil salad cream

If you can get hold of a basket of multicoloured heritage tomatoes, this salad is a riot of summer colours and flavours. Even if all of your tomatoes are red, the purples of the sage flowers, allium flowers and purple basil leaves make for a very pretty plateful.

**Serves 4**

**For the basil salad cream**

Yolks of 2 hard-boiled eggs

1 teaspoon English mustard

1 tablespoon caster sugar

Juice of ½ lemon

150ml double cream

150ml olive oil

3 tablespoons white wine vinegar

A good handful of basil leaves, roughly chopped

Sea salt and freshly ground black pepper

**For the salad**

6 large ripe tomatoes, cut into slices

6 cherry tomatoes, cut into slices

Extra virgin olive oil

A handful of sage flowers

A handful of allium flowers

A few tips of purple basil

1. First make the salad cream. Mash the egg yolks with a fork in the bottom of a large bowl and add the mustard, sugar and lemon juice. When this has formed a smooth paste, start to whisk in the double cream, then add the oil and vinegar. Switch to a hand-held electric whisk and whip until smooth and thick, then stir in the basil leaves. Taste and add salt and pepper. Store in the fridge until needed.

2. Arrange all the tomato slices on a serving platter, drizzle over a little extra virgin olive oil and sprinkle over the flowers and leaves and some salt and pepper. Serve with the salad cream.

# Chive-printed linguine with purple asparagus, crab & brown butter

Incorporating flowers (or herbs or seeds, for that matter) into the very fabric of homemade pasta makes for quite beautiful results, and it's worth the trouble for the occasional special meal. Chive flowers, purple asparagus and crab are all at their best over the same few short weeks, and luckily they all rub along very happily.

**Serves 4**

**For the pasta**

400g '00' pasta flour, plus extra for dusting

4 large eggs

2 tablespoons extra virgin olive oil

Sea salt and freshly ground black pepper

A few handfuls of chive flowers, broken into florets

**For the brown butter**

75g salted butter

Juice of ½ lemon

**For the crab and asparagus**

500g purple asparagus, tough ends removed

Extra virgin olive oil

The white meat from 1 dressed crab (don't waste the brown meat – eat it as a snack spread on toast with butter, lemon juice and plenty of pepper)

1. In a large bowl, mix all of the pasta ingredients together, except the chive flowers, with a wooden spoon and then use your hands to form a dough. On a lightly floured surface, knead the dough until smooth, around 10 minutes. Wrap the dough in clingfilm and rest it in the fridge for at least 30 minutes.

2. While it is resting, make the brown butter by heating the butter slowly in a saucepan until the whey gathers at the bottom. Within a few minutes it will cook and turn brown and at this point, squeeze the lemon into it and take it off the heat. It can be made ahead of time and heated through at the last minute.

3. Cut the pasta dough into four pieces and roll out each piece into a shape that is roughly as wide as your pasta machine. Feed it through on the widest setting, and then take it down a notch and repeat until you have reached the third notch. Set aside, covered in clingfilm, and repeat with the other pieces.

4. Take two pieces of pasta and lay them out next to each other. Set aside a handful of the chive florets for finishing the dish, then sprinkle half of the remainder across one pasta sheet, and lay the other sheet on top, pressing down lightly all over. Set the pasta machine back to its widest setting and feed the sandwiched pair through, again incrementally taking it down to about notch three. You will find the pasta is too delicate to go to the thinnest setting. Add the ribbon-cutting attachment and feed it through again, or cut ribbons by hand with a sharp knife. Hang the ribbons over a wire coat hanger and then make the second batch. Set a pan of water boiling ready to cook it.

5. Place a griddle onto your stove top and while it is heating slice the asparagus tips in half and drop them into a bowl with a

little extra virgin olive oil. Turn the spears over in the oil so that they are well coated and then lay them onto the hot griddle. After a few minutes check to see if black griddle lines have appeared, and when they have, turn the spears over and cook the other side.

6. Meanwhile, reheat the brown butter and tip the white crab meat in to heat it through. Put the pasta into the boiling water for a couple of minutes. Test, and drain when ready. Divide the pasta among individual bowls, put the asparagus spears on top of the pasta, pour the crab and butter over and then sprinkle with the remaining chive flowers. Serve hot.

# Rosemary creams

I first made these to create a more herbal (and less sickly) alternative to old-fashioned rose and violet creams and because I wanted to find a happy place to combine rosemary flowers and dark chocolate. They make a lovely Christmas present, rosemary being one of the few edible flowers that is blooming in the middle of winter. You will need a sugar/chocolate thermometer to make these.

**Makes about 20**

20 crystallised rosemary flowers
(see page 18)

200g dark chocolate (no higher than 70 per cent cocoa)

**For the fondant centre**

300g white sugar

75ml water

¼ teaspoon cream of tartar

1 teaspoon liquid glucose

1 sprig of rosemary

Small cupful of fresh rosemary flowers

1. First make the fondant centre. Put the sugar, water, cream of tartar, glucose and rosemary sprig into a saucepan and bring to the boil without stirring. Cook until it reaches soft-ball stage, 112°C. Remove the sprig of rosemary and discard, then pour the mixture out onto a cool surface, ideally a marble worktop or slab. It will be extremely hot and very runny at first. Use a spatula to push the mixture towards the centre and to start working it as it cools. As you work the fondant it will slowly start to turn white and stiffer and may eventually crumble apart. Test whether it is cool enough to work with your hands. It is at this stage that you should sprinkle on the fresh rosemary flowers and work them in: any sooner and they will lose their lovely purple colour and turn brown. Wrap the fondant in clingfilm and leave to cool. When it is completely cool, shape the fondant into small rounds and set on greaseproof paper.

2. Next you need to temper your chocolate, which is a faff but absolutely worth it for shine and snap. Break off a chunk of chocolate and set it aside, then melt the rest of the chocolate in a bowl set over a pan of gently simmering water until it reaches between 46–49°C. Remove the bowl from the heat and drop in the chunk of chocolate, then stir constantly until the chocolate reaches around 27°C. Next, set the bowl back over the pan of gently simmering water and bring the temperature up to between 31–32°C. (Do be aware that if the temperature rises above 32°C you will have to start again; if it gets below 31°C you can just gently warm it up again.) Dip your pieces of rosemary cream in the chocolate, place them back onto the greaseproof paper and place a crystallised rosemary flower onto the top of each one and leave to set.

# Chamomile lawn cocktail

This is an aromatic and sparkling cocktail for a summer's day.

**Serves 8**

Chamomile syrup made with 2 cups each of water, sugar and chamomile flowers (see page 106)

450ml pressed apple juice

750ml prosecco

1. Make the syrup the day before and then make sure it and the other components are well chilled right up until the moment of combining and serving.

2. Fill each glass with around one-third syrup and one-third apple juice and then top it up with prosecco.

# Omelette tourangelle with oregano flowers

A herby omelette traditionally made with a mix of tarragon, parsley, chervil and chives, mine always majors in oregano.

**Serves 2**

**For the sauce**

10 large tomatoes, halved

2 onions, quartered

1 sprig of rosemary

Olive oil, for drizzling

A couple of sprigs of oregano

**For the omelette**

5 large eggs

A good handful of chopped oregano, tarragon, parsley, chervil, chives or any other leafy herbs you have to hand

Sea salt and freshly ground black pepper

A knob of butter

60g log of semi-soft goat's cheese, sliced

A small handful of oregano flowers and leaves, to garnish

1. Preheat your oven to 190°C/gas mark 5.

2. Place the tomatoes cut-side up in a roasting tin with the onions and rosemary, drizzle with the oil, then scatter over the oregano. Roast for 40–50 minutes, or until the edges of the tomatoes and onions are caramelising. Remove the rosemary, tip the vegetables into a food-processor and pulse to make a chunky, rich sauce. Warm through in a small saucepan ready for serving.

3. To make the omelette, whisk together the eggs, herbs and a pinch each of salt and pepper. Heat the butter in a small frying pan over a moderate heat until it bubbles and then quiets. Pour in the egg mixture. Let it cook for a few seconds then pull the sides into the middle to create a mound of cooked egg, letting the uncooked egg run out to the edges. Lay the goat's cheese slices along the centre. Lift the omelette a little and as soon as it has started to brown nicely, flip the two sides over the cheese.

4. Serve immediately with a few spoonfuls of the roasted tomato sauce, topped with the oregano flowers and leaves.

# Lavender & honey-basted lamb chops

Lamb and lavender are traditional partners in Provençal cooking, the lavender lending a sweetness to the rich meat. Basting the chops with a basting brush made from a sprig of lavender transfers just the right amount of flavour.

**Serves 4**

4 lamb chops

8 tablespoons  honey

8–10 lavender flowers, stalks tied, plus one extra head for the marinade

1. The night before you plan to cook, put the lamb chops into an airtight container and pour on 4 tablespoons of the honey, then break up the single flower head and add it, too, turning everything over with your hands so that the honey, lavender and meat are all in good contact. Leave to marinate in the fridge overnight.

2. The following day, heat a barbecue to white coals and place the chops on the grill. Dip the lavender basting brush into the remaining honey and use it to help keep the meat coated and moist, turning the brush and repeating plenty of times so that the oils from the lavender are released. Cook both sides until browned, brushing all the time.

# Floral & herbal oils & vinegars

By infusing oils and vinegars with petals, leaves and seeds, you create new vehicles for these flavours from the garden. Vinegars and oils can be poured onto salads, of course, but also stirred in as a last layer of flavour in a slow-cooked stew or dish of lentils, or included in a sauce or marinade for fish or chicken.

Infuse a handful of jasmine flowers in rice vinegar (far left in the photo) and then sprinkle onto boiled rice or stir-fries, or use in marinades for fish. The jasmine flowers make for a delicate and aromatic vinegar. Chive vinegar (far right) is one of the most commonly made and widely used, the chive flowers turning the vinegar a strong pink over time, as the colour and the flavour leaves the petals and transfers to the liquid. You can then use it to make a lightly chive-flavoured vinaigrette with a faint blush, or adapt the salad cream recipe on page 54 to make a delicately pink chive salad cream. Strips of lemon zest and sprigs of thyme (second right) will infuse into a vinegar that would make a good addition to a marinade for chicken in particular.

Making flavoured vinegars is pretty straightforward: choose your vinegar, choose your flavouring and put the two together. Steep the infused vinegar for a week or two before you start using.

Oils are slightly more complex, in that there is some significant danger in leaving wet ingredients in oil for very long. The oil creates an airless environment in which botulism can grow. It is very rare for people to pick up botulism infections, but when they do it is usually fatal. So the best plan is to create flavoured oils in small batches that you use quickly. A chilli and rosemary oil (third left) is very good indeed on pizzas and in robust pasta sauces. Heat the oil gently, slice up the chillies and lightly chop the rosemary then pour the warm oil over them. Heat gently for a few minutes, then leave the oil to cool, strain off the chilli and rosemary and use. For a stronger-tasting oil, grind the chilli and rosemary in a little oil first and then cook and strain. Petals ground into oils can make especially beautiful ingredients. Borage makes a savoury oil with blue specks (second left), good for dressing a salad, while calendula petals will turn the oil a golden orange (third right). Use it to give paellas and stews a golden sheen.

# *Leaf*

Dill, basil, parsley, chervil, coriander, banana leaf,
turmeric leaf, wasabi leaf, lemongrass, kaffir lime leaf,
ginger leaf, fig leaf, blackcurrant leaf, peach leaf, vine
leaf, bay, scented geranium, lemon verbena, mint,
rosemary, tarragon.

# Annual herbs

When we think of cooking with leaves it is annual herbs that spring most readily to mind. Bite for bite, these are some of the strongest, punchiest flavours you can produce in the garden. And there is no requirement to draw out the flavours of tough old leaves by means of infusing; being annuals they only last one year, so are always tender and appetising.

### Dill

Delicate, ferny dill tastes a little of aniseed, a little of fennel, though perhaps it is sweeter than both. It is most at home in the foods of Eastern Europe, Russia and Scandinavia, but I am a fan and use it everywhere: in salads, on scrambled eggs, over lentils and roast vegetables and more.

It is not the easiest of annuals to grow, perhaps because the plants hate to be moved, so the seed really needs to be sown direct into the ground where you want it to grow after frosts have receded and the soil has warmed enough to encourage germination. Dill often runs to flower quickly from a spring sowing, so try sowing it after midsummer, too, when it can bulk up much more successfully and often keep going into winter with only a little protection. Dill is a herb that is worth growing because it is at its best when fresh and really loses its flavour when dried.

### Basil

Savoury, peppery and with a hint of anise, basil is the gateway herb; the one herb we can expect our children to munch on in great quantities via pesto pasta. Freshly made pesto highlights all of basil's many charms, but it is beautiful in un-pestled state, too – especially when teamed with its soulmate, the sun-ripened tomato, with which it connects on an almost molecular level.

Sweet basil (*Ocimum basilicum* 'Genovese') is perhaps the most delicious and certainly the most ubiquitous variety available in the shops, but it is not the easiest to grow, hating the ups and downs in temperature that come with a spring sowing and rotting off at the drop of an overwatering or a cold night. Start this variety in a heated propagator and coddle it indoors until the nights are warm, then plant it out with perhaps the protection of a cloche. Far easier to grow is Greek basil (*Ocimum obovatum*), which has tiny, strongly flavoured leaves and a bushy habit. But once you have mastered basil propagation you can also try the complex minty and peppery Thai basil (*O. basilicum* var. *thyrsiflora*), citrusy lemon basil (*O.* × *citriodorum*) and spicy holy basil (*O. tenuiflorum*).

## Parsley

Strictly speaking parsley is a biennial, as it completes its life cycle over two seasons, but it is grown as an annual, so in this section it stays. It certainly has the munchable and strongly flavoured leaves boasted by all of the annual herbs. For many years white and insipid parsley sauce rather put me off parsley, but I have come back to it as a brightener: it is brilliant scattered over salads or – perhaps even better – over slow-cooked dishes, the welcome flash of fresh green. It also is the primary ingredient in piquant and vibrant salsa verde, and there are few dishes that aren't improved by a blob of that.

The only decision you need to make when growing it is whether to go for the flat-leaved or curly variety. Flat-leaved has generally overtaken curly as the culinary parsley du jour, and its texture is certainly more appealing, but there are those who prefer the stronger, iron-rich flavour of curly parsley. I have had best results when sowing parsley after midsummer, ideally into pots and then planted out in late summer or early autumn. It is pretty hardy and will provide you with leaves right through until spring, though they will be softer and less weatherbeaten if grown under cover, such as a cloche or a sheltered window box, or even in a polytunnel.

## Chervil

Chervil is parsley's refined and elegant cousin. It has a broadly similar flavour but it is subtler and gentler, with more of a hint of aniseed. The texture of the leaf is soft and ferny. It is a gorgeous lacy thing. Sow seeds direct where you would like them to grow – the plants don't like to be disturbed – making sowings in both spring and just after late summer. Spring sowings should be made somewhere shady and cool, as hot sun will quickly send plants to flower and seed. Make sure you sow fresh seed: old seed will not germinate. Chervil is at its greatest in quickly cooked egg dishes: in France it is one of the '*fines herbes*' (along with parsley, tarragon and chives) used in omelette aux fines herbes, and it is equally good over scrambled eggs. It quickly loses its delicate flavour when heated, so use chervil leaves either raw or lightly cooked.

## Coriander

Pungent, earthy coriander is hard to miss in a dish. This is a love/hate herb and some people find the flavour unbearably soapy and harsh. Personally, I like it – but in small quantities, sprinkled sparsely over something more comforting such as a dhal or a chilli con carne. It is essential in Mexican and Tex-Mex dishes and widely used in Indian, Chinese and Thai cuisines.

Sow in spring or after midsummer directly into the place where you want it to grow, and choose a shady spot for spring sowings. Bolting (plants quickly running to flower and seed) is almost always a problem when growing coriander, so do look out for slow-bolting cultivars such as 'Slow Bolt'. I have always had better luck with sowings made from midsummer to late summer, which provide leaves all winter long if the plants are kept slightly sheltered.

# Beetroot & dill cured salmon with dill yogurt

This is one of the places where dill is at its most comfortable – teamed with salmon and beetroot to make a beautiful piece of red-tinged cured fish. It is a great showcase for dill's sweet aniseedy herbiness.

**Serves 8–10**

**For the fish**

800g salmon fillet

1 tablespoon fine salt

3 tablespoons granulated sugar

30g dill, finely chopped

Zest of 1 lime

2 raw beetroots, washed and grated

**For the yogurt sauce**

4 tablespoons Greek yogurt

1 tablespoon chopped dill

1 teaspoon chopped capers

Sea salt and freshly ground black pepper

1. Rinse the fillet and pat it dry, then check it all over for small pin bones, pulling them out with a pair of tweezers. Take a sharp knife and trim off the belly – the thinner part that runs along one side. Slice the fillet in half and place one piece into a dish across which you have laid a long piece of clingfilm. Shake ½ tablespoon of salt and 1½ tablespoons sugar across the thick central parts of each fillet. Mix the dill and the lime zest together and scatter half of this mixture across the fillet in the dish. Next, lay all of the grated beetroot along this fillet's length and top it with the rest of the dill mixture, and then the other piece of fish, salted and sugared side facing down. Now start to wrap the fillets tightly in the clingfilm, trying to encourage the top piece of fish into full contact with the bottom piece. Lay out another piece of clingfilm lengthways and wrap it around the fish several times. Place the package back into the dish and into the fridge. You will need to leave it to cure now for two days, but turn the fish twice each day, once in the morning and once in the evening.

2. When you are ready to serve, unwrap the fish and scrape back most of the cure, leaving some dill behind. Slice the fish thinly on an angle. Mix all of the yogurt sauce ingredients together and serve with slices of salmon and dark rye bread.

# Orange & parsley gremolata with beef & orange stew

Gremolata is an Italian condiment made of a finely chopped mix of herbs, lemon zest and garlic. It is used to liven up slow-cooked meats, grilled fish or chicken, and to give them a zing of aromatic freshness. This one is made with orange zest instead of lemon and is lovely with rich meat. The stew is best made the day before and reheated; the gremolata should be freshly made.

**Serves 4**

**For the stew**

2 tablespoons vegetable oil

1 onion, chopped

6 garlic cloves, sliced

750g braising steak, cut into 4cm chunks

2 tablespoons flour

2 slices pancetta, diced

350g carrots, cut into chunky pieces

2 bay leaves

A few sprigs thyme – use orange thyme if you have it

500ml stout

300ml water

Zest and juice of 1 orange

**For the gremolata**

A bunch of parsley (to make about two tablespoons when chopped)

1 garlic clove

Zest of 1 orange, pared off with a sharp knife (take as little white pith as possible)

1 teaspoon sea salt

1. Heat the oil in a large, heavy-bottomed casserole and fry the onion until it starts to take on a little colour. Add the garlic and cook for a further few minutes, then remove everything from the pan and set aside. Lay the meat out on a plate and sprinkle it with the flour, turning it with your hands so that as many sides as possible are coated. Brown the meat in the pan in batches, then lift it out and set aside. In the same pan, fry the pancetta until it is crispy and then return the meat, onions and garlic to the pan, plus the carrots, bay leaves and thyme. Pour on the stout and water and add the orange zest and juice. Bring to the boil and then simmer on a very low heat, with the lid on slightly askew to allow for evaporation, for around 2 hours. The liquid will slowly become less watery and turn into a thick, rich, dark brown sauce. Remove from the heat and leave to rest, overnight if you can.

2. The next day, reheat the meat just before serving. While it is heating through, finely chop the parsley, garlic and orange zest and mix with the salt. Portion out the stew, sprinkle with the gremolata and serve with chunks of bread to mop up the juices.

# Salsa verde with lemon roast chicken

There are few sauces more useful than salsa verde, which has the piquancy of a ketchup yet the herbal freshness of a pesto. I sometimes hand-chop the ingredients to create a rustic sauce, but I also like to whizz all of the ingredients together in a food-processor. It creates quite a different look, turning the herbs into a vibrant pool of chlorophyll! Make salsa verde part of your repertoire and use it with sausages, chops, roast vegetables and, of course, chicken.

**Serves 2**

4 chicken thighs

10 garlic cloves

1 lemon, cut into quarters

2 tablespoons olive oil

Sea salt and freshly ground black pepper

**For the salsa verde**

The leaves from 1 large bunch parsley

The leaves from 1 small bunch basil

A handful of mint leaves

1 tablespoon capers

6 anchovy fillets

3 tablespoons red wine vinegar

8 tablespoons extra virgin olive oil

1 garlic clove

Sea salt and freshly ground black pepper

1. Preheat your oven to 210°C/gas mark 7.

2. Put the chicken thighs, garlic and lemon into an ovenproof dish and coat everything in the oil. Turn the chicken skin-side up and then sprinkle on the salt and pepper. Bake for 30 minutes then turn the temperature down to 180°C/gas mark 4 and cook for a further 20 minutes, or until the juices run clear and the internal temperature is 77°C when tested with a meat thermometer.

3. Put the ingredients for the salsa verde into a food-processor and blitz until bright green (or chop by hand for a rougher texture).

4. Serve the chicken thighs with the roasted lemon and garlic and a dollop of fresh salsa verde.

# Peach melba with mint & basil sugar

You may think a classic dish such as Peach Melba can't be improved, but in my humble opinion you would be wrong. Both mint and basil are most frequently used as savoury herbs but they both complement fruit beautifully. If the peaches are perfectly ripe and dripping with juice don't bother poaching them, but if they are even slightly disappointing a few minutes simmering in a basil syrup will turn them yieldingly soft with a gorgeous hint of summery herbs.

**Serves 4**

750ml water

750g sugar

Large bunch of basil

Pared zest of 1 lemon

1 vanilla pod, split

4 peaches, halved and stoned

**For the raspberry sauce**

350g raspberries

25g icing sugar

Juice of ½ lemon

**For the basil and mint sugar**

Small bunch of mint (about 15 leaves)

Small bunch of basil (about 30 leaves, when picked from the stems)

2 tablespoons granulated sugar

**To serve**

Good-quality vanilla ice cream

100g raspberries

1. Put the water and sugar into a large saucepan and heat, stirring, until the sugar dissolves and the liquid looks clear. Add the whole stalks of basil, the pared lemon zest and the vanilla pod and simmer for 10 minutes. Lower the peaches carefully into the simmering syrup and poach for a few minutes on each side. Test them for tenderness with a knife point, and if just cooked, lift them out with a slotted spoon. Leave to cool.

2. Meanwhile, make the raspberry sauce by blending together the raspberries, icing sugar and lemon juice and pushing the mixture through a sieve.

3. In a pestle and mortar, bash together the mint, basil and sugar until the leaves have disintegrated and the sugar has turned green.

4. Place two peach halves on each serving dish with a scoop of ice cream and a few raspberries, then pour over a little raspberry sauce and sprinkle over the herb sugar.

# Basil limeade

A refreshing, citrusy and herbal summer drink. Add vodka to turn it into a grown-up tipple.

**Makes 6 glasses**

400ml water

350g caster sugar

Large bunch of basil

Ice cubes

Juice of 12 limes

500ml sparkling water, chilled

1. In a saucepan, heat the water and the sugar until the sugar dissolves, then bring to the boil, add half of the basil, stalks and all, and simmer for 10 minutes. Transfer to a bowl and leave to cool completely. Once cool, cover and refrigerate.

2. Place the remaining basil stalks into the bottom of a large jug and bash them a little with a wooden spoon. Add the ice cubes to the jug and pour over the chilled syrup and the lime juice and mix well, then top up with the sparkling water. Serve over ice cubes.

# Chervil butter & chervil salt with radishes

Soft and aniseedy chervil makes an intensely savoury herb butter as well
as a fragrant dipping salt for enjoying the first radishes of the year.

**Serves 4, as a starter**

A few radishes each, cleaned
and trimmed

**For the butter**

50g salted butter, softened

1 tablespoon finely chopped chervil

Sea salt

**For the dipping salt**

1 tablespoon flaky sea salt

2 tablespoons finely chopped chervil

1. For the butter, mix the butter, chervil and salt well, transfer to
   a small dish, cover and chill in the fridge.

2. For the dipping salt, reserve a couple of pinches of salt and then
   combine the remainder of the salt and the chervil in a pestle
   and mortar. Grind it together, tip it into a small bowl and stir
   through the unground salt flakes.

3. Serve the butter and dipping salt with the clean radishes to cut,
   spread and dip.

# Tabbouleh-style winter salad

I love the Middle Eastern tradition of using herb leaves as salad leaves in great, generous mouth-filling quantities, rather than as the odd fleck. Tabbouleh is the ultimate herb-leaf salad, more parsley than anything else. A traditional tabbouleh is a summer salad of parsley, mint and tomatoes, but as I always have parsley in greatest quantities in winter I have slowly ended up with this wintery version.

**Serves 4**

30g medium bulgar wheat

175g parsley, leaves separated from the stem and finely chopped

A couple of mint sprigs, leaves finely chopped

6 cauliflower florets, stalks cut off and broken into tiny mini florets

10 radishes, roughly chopped

80ml extra virgin olive oil

Zest and juice of 1 lemon

Sea salt and freshly ground black pepper

1. Put the bulgar wheat into a heatproof jug and pour over just-boiled water to over twice the depth of the grain. Leave for 20 minutes, then drain.

2. Combine the drained bulgar wheat with all the remaining ingredients in a large bowl and leave to sit for 10 minutes before serving.

# Pestos & salsa verdes

Pound together herbs, hard cheese, nuts and oil and the result is more than the sum of its parts. Pesto releases the magic in basil, the other ingredients rendering it satisfying and savoury.

*Pesto alla Genovese* (3) – originating in the Ligurian port of Genoa – strictly comprises sweet or Genovese basil ('Genovese'), pine nuts, Parmesan or pecorino cheese, garlic, olive oil and salt. If you have only ever tried it from a jar then you are missing out. Pound garlic and pine nuts up in a pestle and mortar until they reach a paste, then add the leaves and salt and pound again, and finally add the finely grated hard cheese and trickle in the oil, until it reaches your desired runniness.

This basic blueprint morphs as you move around the Mediterranean coast. In Provence, where they are less abundant, pine nuts are dropped to make *pistou* (4), a basil sauce used as a finishing touch on *soupe au pistou*, which is similar to minestrone. The *pistou* is added as a fragrant and fresh herby dollop, just before serving.

*Salsa verde* (1) obtains its savouriness via anchovies rather than cheese. Chop equal parts parsley, mint and basil, pound with a couple of anchovy fillets, a teaspoon of capers, a little Dijon mustard and a splash of vinegar, then loosen with extra virgin olive oil. Its sharpness makes *salsa verde* wonderful with fatty sausages or chops, but likewise with delicate fish and seafood. It is the traditional accompaniment to *bollito misto*, a slow-cooked stew of various meats. I am telling you to pound, and that is the way to go if you want a rustic texture but of course you can make slicker versions in seconds in a blender: just do pulse rather than not.

*Salsa alla dragoncello* (2) hails from Siena, and comprises handfuls of tarragon (*dragoncello*) pounded with breadcrumbs, garlic, lemon juice and olive oil. Its sharp aniseed herbiness is beautiful with roast chicken.

Pesto's more exotic cousins can generally trace their origins to Mediterranean migrations: Portuguese settlers in Singapore are thought to be behind *laksa pesto* (5), which comprises coriander, cashew nuts and fish sauce, the latter providing the umami note usually supplied by the cheese. And *chimmichurri*, the Argentinean herb sauce made from parsley, oregano, garlic, oil and vinegar, may have followed Basque settlers.

The blueprint provides permission to mess about: a woodland pesto of nettles, toasted hazelnuts and hard goat's cheese; a fragrant chervil, toasted almond and pecorino version. Whatever green herb you have to hand – even strong-tasting leaves such as watercress and rocket – precedent suggests that it is going to taste pretty marvellous mashed up with some garlic, cheese, nuts and olive oil.

# Exotic leaves

Admittedly these are not the easiest of crops, but they are not as tricky as you would imagine either. You do not need to be gardening in the tropics in order to grow any of them, but there is a trick to successful cultivation, and it is to discard any thoughts of growing these plants in the traditional way – for their roots or their fruits – and just go all out for the flavours held captive in the leaves. Picked fresh from the plant, they are particularly useful in adding authentic flavours to recipes from the Far East and India.

### Banana

You have no hope of making a banana bear fruit in anything other than a tropical climate, but you can grow the leaves, and easily too. These are subtle in flavour but are wonderful for wrapping and cooking delicate ingredients such as fish, to which they impart a gentle, grassy, vegetable flavour. In temperate climes choose the hardy banana, *Musa basjoo*, which hails from Japanese mountain areas and so is resistant to frost. It can be planted straight out into the garden. It is a good idea to wrap its stems in hessian or bubblewrap for its first couple of winters, but beyond that it will be big and tough enough to see itself through, dying back to the ground each winter and springing forth again each spring. Harvest the leaves as soon as they are the size you want them.

### Turmeric

Growing turmeric is a recent discovery for me, but it has quickly leapfrogged high onto my list of must-have plants. You won't grow anything much in the way of the root-like part (in fact a rhizome) that you would normally use in cooking, but you will get plenty of leaves, and these are something very special. They are traditionally used in a Goan dumpling dish called patholi, wrapped around coconut and jaggery dumplings and then steamed. Do this once and you will be hooked, as the scent that wafts through the house on steaming is truly beautiful, floral and citrusy with a hint of spice. This flavour penetrates the dumplings, and indeed can be extracted by infusing gently in milk or syrup. It is hard to find plants of turmeric, and I grow my own from rhizomes bought at a local Thai supermarket. They need warmth and plenty of time to sprout, and I have had best results by potting them up in compost and keeping them warm and moist in a heated propagator over several weeks. Thereafter, treat them as a houseplant, albeit one that has a summer holiday outside in the garden every year.

### Wasabi

The nose-burningly fiery swollen stems of the wasabi plant – the traditional accompaniment to the gentle mildness of a piece of sushi or sashimi – have since time immemorial been grown in the stream edges of Japanese mountains: they need these perfect conditions for the swollen stems to bulk up. They are hardy plants so if you have a well-shaded clean water stream yourself you can certainly have a shot at growing them for the stems. But in the event that you don't, grow them for the leaves. The plants fare very happily in a pot of soil or in the ground and will produce good looking leaves in spring and autumn: the leaves turn yellow in the heat of summer, and die down in winter. They taste much like wasabi, but sweeter and gentler, and make a beautiful salad leaf.

### Lemongrass

Lemongrass is fragrant, sharp and citrusy and bestrides the worlds of sweet and savoury. The woody 'bulbs' from the base of the grass are widely available from shops of course but when grown in your own garden those flavours are that bit fresher. I just bought a couple of the bulbs from the shops and pushed them into the earth. In a pot in a sunny spot my lemongrass doesn't grow especially fast, it is slow to bulk up and spread, which leaves me reluctant to pull whole plants out of the ground and use them in the traditional way. However, I do often nip out the green leafy tips of the plant, which have always been cut off when you buy it from the grocer or supermarket. These are softer and sweeter than the woodier base of the plant and can be eaten (they are good in curry pastes), rather than simply used for flavouring. Keep plants in a frost-free place over winter.

### Kaffir lime

It would be a delight to be able to produce knobbly-skinned, aromatic kaffir lime fruits in cooler climates, but even in the countries where they ripen easily it is the leaves that are most sought out for cooking. And here we all get lucky, for with a little care we can grow plenty of leaves. Glossy, dark green and hour-glass shaped, they are intensely fragrant: lemony, limey with a hint of spice. Kaffir lime plants are not widely sold but can be bought from specialist citrus nurseries. I grow mine as a house plant in winter and a patio plant in summer and pick off the leaves as and when I need them. They are wonderful in a fragrant Asian bouquet garni with lemongrass and ginger leaves, as the base for soups.

### Ginger

Just as with turmeric, don't bother growing this for the rhizome, which will only increase in size incrementally in temperate areas. But do grow it for the leaves, which have a gentle, fresh ginger flavour and are brilliant chopped up for stir-fries, curries or tisanes. I would grow using rhizomes from the supermarket and a heated propagator.

# Coconut & turmeric leaf sweet rice pudding with griddled mango

Turmeric leaf's sweet, spicy, citrus flavour needs to be drawn gently out. This coconut milk pudding is the ideal vehicle for this. You will be glad you went to the trouble, and your house will be beautifully scented throughout the long, slow cooking.

**Serves 4**

**For the rice pudding**

80g pudding rice

65g jaggery (or substitute dark muscovado sugar)

400ml coconut milk

400ml water

6 turmeric leaves

1 vanilla pod, split

50ml double cream

**For the mango**

2 ripe mangoes

1 lime, quartered

1. For the pudding, heat your oven to 150°C/gas mark 2. Choose a casserole dish that is as happy on the stove top as in the oven, and tip in all of the ingredients. Bring to the boil on the hob, stir well and then place in the oven. Bake for at least 1 hour 30 minutes, stirring several times, and remove from the heat when the rice is tender. Just before serving, remove the turmeric leaves and the vanilla pods from the rice pudding.

2. Take a sharp knife and slice off the 'cheeks' of the mangoes, carefully sliding the knife either side of the stone as you cut. Slip each piece out of its skin, then slice it once, lengthways. Heat a griddle and lay a piece of mango across it until black marks are seared into it, turn and griddle the peak of the other domed side, then repeat again for the cut side. Repeat for each piece of mango.

3. Spoon the pudding into bowls, place two pieces of hot mango on top and squeeze over the lime juice.

# Tempura wasabi with dipping sauce

Once you start deep-frying leaves in tempura batter it is difficult to stop. All annual herb leaves in particular are great, and difficult to resist when transformed into impressively spiky, crunchy versions of themselves, frozen in the moment. Use your larger and older wasabi leaves for this, as they are stronger in taste than the little ones, and the flavour is slightly dampened by the cooking.

**Serves 4–6**

1 teaspoon salt

100g rice flour

175ml pale ale

Vegetable oil, for deep-frying

Wasabi leaves, a few per person

**For the dipping sauce**

3 tablespoons soy sauce

2 teaspoons rice wine vinegar

1 teaspoon sesame oil

1 teaspoon caster sugar

1. Put the salt and flour into a large bowl and whisk in the ale, then leave at room temperature for 10 minutes.

2. Meanwhile, whisk together all the ingredients for the dipping sauce and set aside.

3. Fill a saucepan a third full of vegetable oil, then heat the oil to 180°C. Take the wasabi leaves a few at a time and dip them into the batter then lower them into the oil. Fry for a couple of minutes then turn them over and do the same on the other side. Lift out with a slotted spoon and drain on kitchen paper, then serve while hot, with the dipping sauce.

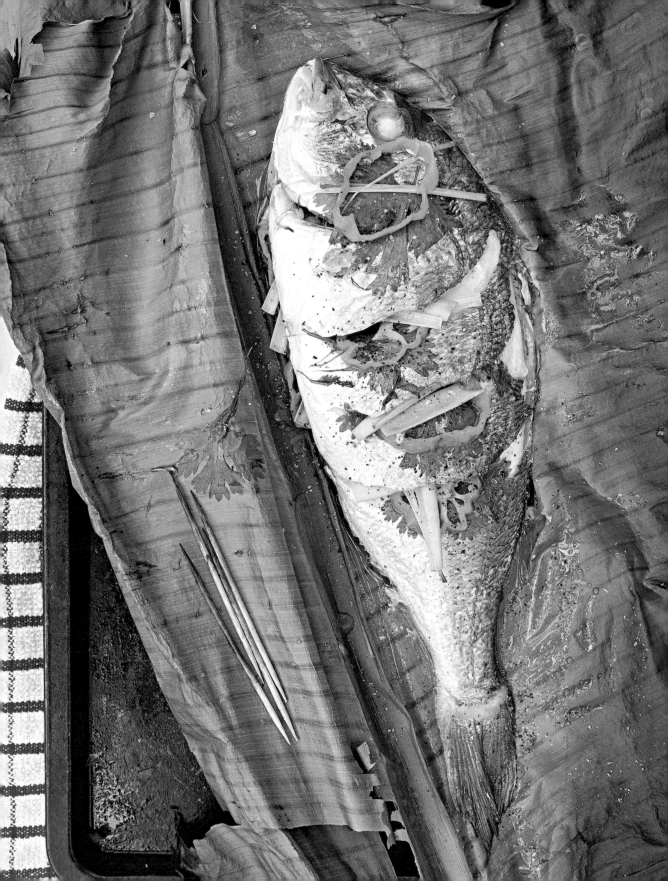

# Banana leaf steamed bream

Use the banana leaf as a living steamer (or at least recently living) in which to trap whichever flavourings you choose to throw in. Its own grassy vegetable flavour penetrates the fish, too. You can find banana leaves in the freezer compartment of oriental supermarkets, but I just machete mine off the plant with a big kitchen knife, which is a fine way to start preparing a meal.

**Serves 2**

1 sea bream, gutted and cleaned

1 banana leaf, cut to about twice the length of the fish (you will also need some cocktail sticks to secure the parcel)

½ lemongrass stalk, cut into slivers

1 chilli, sliced into rounds (deseeded if you want more flavour than heat)

A handful of coriander leaves

1. Preheat the oven to 220°C/gas mark 7.

2. Lay the fish onto one half of the banana leaf and make three cuts into the fish flesh with a sharp knife, diagonally into its side. Fill each slash with a few shards of lemongrass stalk, a round or two of chilli and a few coriander leaves. Turn the fish over and repeat on the other side, then put a little of each of the flavourings into the belly cavity.

3. Wrap the fish tightly in the banana leaf – I have found that cocktail sticks work really well to secure these parcels, but you might prefer to tie it with butcher's twine. Place the parcel on a baking tray and cook on a high oven shelf for 25 minutes. (This recipe also works really well on a barbecue; just place the parcel directly onto the grill and cook for around 25 minutes.)

4. Unwrap the parcels at the table and eat immediately, straight from the leaf.

# Tom yum soup

This is the way to really appreciate your exotic leaves. Tom yum soup is essentially a stock, made from all of the most aromatic of flavours: the fragrant leaves become part of a sort of Asian bouquet garni. It is also hot and sour and almost certainly the cure for whatever may ail you.

**Serves 4**

20 raw prawns, with shell on

Vegetable oil, for frying

1 litre water

6 kaffir lime leaves, roughly chopped

2 lemongrass stalks, roughly chopped

2 ginger leaves, roughly chopped

2 Thai basil stalks

2 red chillies, deseeded and sliced

1 tablespoon caster sugar

Juice of 1 lime

1½ tablespoons fish sauce

A few coriander leaves, to garnish

1. Remove the prawn meat from the shells and set it aside, then put a little oil in the bottom of a large saucepan and fry the shells until they turn pink. Pour on the water and bring to the boil. Simmer for a few minutes then pour the stock through a sieve into another bowl. Discard the shells and pour the stock back into the pan, adding the lime leaves, lemongrass, ginger leaves, Thai basil, chillies and sugar, then bring back to the boil and simmer for 10 minutes. Drop in the prawn meat and cook until pink, then take the pan off the heat and add the lime juice and fish sauce.

2. Divide the prawns between four bowls, top with the stock and garnish with a few coriander leaves.

# Tisanes

A tisane is the simplest way in which to draw out the flavours of the garden. If you are already a drinker of herbal teas (and even if you are not), look beyond the dusty teabags in the cupboard and venture out into the garden. There are leaves, seeds and petals that make beautiful clear and fragrant teas; the flavour is in a different league. Simply pour freshly boiled water onto a few leaves, seeds or petals and then enjoy the vibrant essential oils as they cloud up to your nose and linger in the cup.

Queen of all of the herbal teas is lemon verbena (4). Just a couple of leaves and a few minutes' steeping makes a drink that tastes like hot, liquid lemon sherbet – sweet without a drop of sugar. Mints are next on my list, fresh mint tea being so very many leagues above dried. Moroccan mint (1) (*Mentha spicata* var. *crispa* 'Moroccan') is the mint traditionally used for teas and is one of the best, being strongly aromatic, but you might also try peppermint (*Mentha × piperita*) or a spearmint such as *Mentha spicata* 'Kentucky Colonel', the correct mint for use in mint juleps but pretty good as a tea, too. Spearmint makes one of the best after-dinner teas, for settling the stomach, while peppermint is good for cooling the mouth after hot food. Leaves of ginger, turmeric and lemongrass all have great flavour and fragrance, as do those of some of the fruit bushes and trees, in particular blackcurrant leaves, which make an oddly blackcurrant-like tea.

Among the petals there are perhaps fewer choices, but all of the herb flowers make lovely tisanes, being slightly more honeyed than their leafy bits, so do try thyme, basil and rosemary flower teas. Chamomile (3) is a flavour that some love, some hate, but if you are keen then do try it fresh, at bedtime, with a spoonful of honey.

Fennel (2) is wonderful as a tea at any stage of its aniseed-scented life – leaf, flower, seed – though I particularly love to catch it halfway between flower and seed. The green seeds make a tea with a lovely balance of grassy, sweet and nutty. Also try angelica seeds and sweet cicely for similarly delicious and anise-tinged tisanes.

# Fruit leaves

We grow fruit trees and bushes for their fleeting, once-a-year harvests, never guessing that there is a second, hidden harvest of flavours trapped in their leaves. Not all of the fruit trees and bushes do this: you can boil an apple leaf for an hour and get nothing from it but a vaguely green smell, but just a few of them yield up scents and flavours that echo or complement the fruit they bear. Even if your fruit harvest fails – as they are wont to do – you will always be able to extract these unusual tastes.

## Fig

These are one of the true treasures of the garden. Pick a leaf and rub it and you get almost nothing, except perhaps a little sticky sap on your fingers. Wrap the leaf around a cheese or piece of fish and bake it, though, or immerse a leaf into a sugar syrup and simmer it and it releases a completely unexpected aroma and flavour – strongly coconutty but with a good hint of elderflower. It's an odd and beautiful flavour and unsurprisingly it complements figs perfectly.

Fig trees are big plants and have alarmingly invasive roots. They also fruit better if their roots are confined. To keep them compact and to encourage best possible fruiting, plant into the biggest pot you can find or dig a pit and line it with concrete paving slabs, fill it with soil and plant into that. They need full sun for best fruit; in the Mediterranean and other warm countries they can produce two crops of fruit a year, but in cooler climates remove any fruits that haven't ripened by the end of the summer. This concentrates energy on the following year's crop. Pick the leaves from spring to autumn (they will drop in autumn) and wipe them down before using. Fig leaves produce a sap when first picked that may prove mildly irritating to some, so watch out for it.

## Blackcurrant

Pick a blackcurrant leaf and crush it and you will know exactly what to expect, flavour wise: blackcurrant – surprise, surprise. The flavour of blackcurrant leaf is more austere than blackcurrant fruit, less luscious and fulsome, and it makes a beautifully sharp and delicate sorbet, or cuts through the creaminess when used in an ice cream.

Plant blackcurrant bushes in autumn or winter. Currants are among the few fruits that will grow well in some shade, though you will get the most abundant and sweetest fruits in full sun. You can pick and use the leaves all season, but they are at their best early in the year.

### Nectarine/peach

Nectarines and peaches are closely related to almonds, and it is this relationship that becomes apparent when you use their leaves in cooking. Strong almond wafts emerge from infusions of peach leaves. They make a good flavouring for custards and ice creams, and can be made into a syrup that can be poured onto fruit or milky desserts, or used as the base for almond-flavoured cocktails.

Both nectarines and peaches need a sunny and sheltered spot in order to produce and ripen fruit, and both suffer from the debilitating peach leaf curl. This is an ugly fungal disease that blows in on early spring rains and will render even the leaves unusable. The trick is to grow both under cover in a greenhouse or polytunnel, or train them against a wall and cover the whole plant in a showerproof covering from late winter until late spring. You can also find dwarf plants of both, which can be grown in pots and moved to safety.

### Grape

Vine leaves are unusual among the fruit tree leaves in that they don't taste of very much themselves. Unusually, too, these leaves are eaten in their entirety, rather than having their flavours extracted and the bulk of the leaf discarded. But vine leaves do have a wonderful ability to turn soft and malleable on cooking, making them excellent vessels for other ingredients. A vine leaf exists for stuffing full of tasty things, steaming until the leaf clings to its filling, and then popping whole into your mouth.

Grapes are big, vigorous plants and you will almost always have plenty of leaves, though they are loveliest in the spring and early summer before unappetising problems such as powdery mildew get a grip. Grow over a sturdy support in full sunlight for good sweet grapes. There are almost always too many leaves, and no problem at all with picking lots for your own needs.

# Fennel & tomato dolmades

All of the flavour of dolmades has to be in the rice filling, which is traditionally chock full of herbs – dried and fresh mint in particular. This is an untraditional tomato and fennel version, but still herby and satisfying.

**Makes about 20 dolmades**

20 vine leaves

3 tablespoons olive oil

1 onion, diced

1 fennel bulb, diced

2 tomatoes, skinned, deseeded and diced

2 tablespoons tomato purée

100g white basmati rice

200ml water

Zest of 1 lemon

2 tablespoons pine nuts, toasted

2 tablespoons fresh mint, chopped

1 tablespoon dried mint

2 tablespoons fresh parsley, chopped

**To steam and serve**

10 vine leaves

3 lemons, 2 sliced into rounds, 1 cut into wedges

240ml water

3 tablespoons extra virgin olive oil

1. Snip the stalks from the 20 vine leaves. Bring a large saucepan of water to the boil and cook the leaves for 5 minutes, then drain and plunge into a bowl of cold water. Drain. If using preserved leaves, rinse them then cook in the boiling water for 2 minutes before draining and refreshing in cold water.

2. Next make the filling. Heat the oil and gently fry the onion and fennel until the onion turns translucent. Add the tomatoes and tomato purée and stir in, then tip in the rice and water and bring to the boil. Reduce the heat, cover with a lid and simmer for about 10 minutes, until the water is absorbed and the rice is tender. Add the lemon zest, pine nuts, fresh mint, dried mint and parsley and stir.

3. Preheat your oven to 170°C/gas mark 3.

4. Use five of the uncooked vine leaves to line a large casserole dish, then cover these with the lemon slices. Lie each cooked vine leaf down with the veiny side up, and place a teaspoon of filling into the centre. Fold up from the base first to just cover the filling, fold each side in and then roll up until you have a little cylinder. Start to pack them into the casserole, nice and snug. When you have stuffed them all, cover them with the other five uncooked vine leaves, and tip in the water and extra virgin olive oil. Cover with a lid and bring to the boil, then transfer to the oven and cook for 1 hour.

5. Remove from the oven and leave to cool completely. Serve with the lemon wedges.

# Barbecued fig-leaf-wrapped ricotta with honey & lavender

The mild ricotta absorbs the flavours of the leaf and the lavender, and solidifies as it cooks to make an unusual and not-too-sweet pudding. If you don't have a barbecue on the go you can cook these under the grill. Credit for this idea must go to Matt Williamson, former chef/owner of the brilliant and much-missed Flinty Red, in Bristol, who suggested it the moment I told him my plan for this book.

**Serves 4**

4 large fig leaves

8 tablespoons ricotta

8 sprigs of lavender

4 figs

Honey, for brushing and serving

1. Wipe and dry the fig leaves and lay them out flat, face up. Spoon 2 tablespoons of ricotta into the centre of each and lay one sprig of lavender on top. Fold over the lobes of the leaf to make a package and secure it with a cocktail stick or two. Place the packages onto a hot barbecue or under a hot grill.

2. Slice the figs in half, paint the cut surfaces with honey and lay them cut-side down on the barbecue, or cut-side up under the grill. Cook the leaf packages for about 5 minutes on each side, or until the leaves are charred and wrinkled. Cook the figs for around 5 minutes in total.

3. Serve each person one package and two fig halves, with honey for drizzling and the leftover lavender florets broken up for sprinkling over.

# Blackcurrant leaf granita with cassis

This simple and sophisticated idea emerged from a conversation with food writer Xanthe Clay, and so I have her to thank for the juxtaposition of sharp, clean blackcurrant leaf granita and juicy boozy fruit. Fittingly, the granita is adapted from a recipe by Mark Diacono, who photographed this book and was also at the table. The alcohol in the cassis quickly starts to melt the granita, forming a sort of grown-up slushie, so pour it into one side of your glass if you want to keep a portion of it as crunchy frozen granita until the end (you do).

**Serves 6**

500ml jug well-packed with blackcurrant leaves

270g caster sugar

700ml water

Juice of 3 lemons

6 shots cassis (1 per serving)

1. Put the leaves, sugar and water into a saucepan and heat gently, stirring to dissolve the sugar, then bring to the boil and simmer gently for a few minutes. Remove from the heat and set aside to cool completely. Add the lemon juice, stir well, then strain into a freezerproof container. The container should be large enough that the syrup only fills it to about a third, and should have a well-fitting lid. Place the container in your freezer and set a timer for an hour later.

2. Remove the granita from the freezer, take a fork and scrape all of the ice from the edges into the centre. Mix it in and return it to the freezer. Set your time for 30 minutes and repeat, and again, and so on, for about 3 hours in total. The granita will be soft and snow-like.

3. At the table, scoop a couple of tablespoonfuls into glass bowls (ideally) and tip on the cassis.

# Roast nectarines with amaretti crumble & nectarine-leaf custard

This is almond upon nectarine upon almond. The soft, yielding roasted nectarines are topped with a crunchy and buttery amaretti topping and then smothered in the almond-scented nectarine-leaf custard.

**Serves 4**

125g amaretti biscuits
200g salted butter, softened
2 tablespoons sliced almonds
6 nectarines, halved and stoned

**For the custard**
500ml full-fat milk
200ml double cream
25 nectarine or peach leaves
125g caster sugar
6 egg yolks

1. Preheat the oven to 180°C/gas mark 4.

2. Put the amaretti biscuits into a plastic bag and bash into chunky pieces with a rolling pin. Pour into a large bowl with the butter and sliced almonds and use a wooden spoon to mix them roughly together.

3. Place the nectarines cut-side up in a baking tray and divide the amaretti mixture between them, leaving a good and nubbly little heap. Bake for 30 minutes, or until the topping is golden brown and the nectarines are tender.

4. To make the custard, pour the milk and cream into a saucepan with the nectarine or peach leaves. Bring to the boil, simmer for a moment, then switch off the heat and leave to sit and infuse for 10 minutes.

5. Put the sugar and egg yolks into a large bowl and whisk them together, then strain in a little of the milk and cream mixture and whisk well, then slowly pour in the rest of it, whisking as you go. Clean out the pan and return the mixture to it. Fill a basin with cold water and have it nearby in case of curdling, then start to slowly heat the milk mixture, stirring continually. After about 10 minutes it should start to thicken. It is ready when you can coat the back of a spoon with the custard and draw a clear line across it with your finger. Watch for curdling and at its first sign remove the pan immediately from the heat and lower it into the cold water, whisking hard. This should save it.

6. Serve three warm peach halves to each person alongside a jug of custard to pour over.

# Infusions

Infusing petals, leaves and seeds magically transfers their flavours to some of the most useful ingredients. Infuse them in milk or cream (3) and dessert possibilities stretch out almost infinitely before you: basil choc chip ice cream, sweet cicely seed pannacotta to serve with baked rhubarb, rose and honey semifreddo, lemon-scented geranium crème anglaise to pour over a summer crumble. Whatever combination of flavour and milk-based dessert you can dream up (crème brûlées, bread and butter puddings, custard tarts, I could go on and on…) can be yours, if you don't mind adding 20 minutes or so onto your basic recipe.

The technique is pretty straightforward. Measure the milk or cream needed for your chosen dessert into a pan and bring to the boil – just. Drop in your petals, leaves or seeds – a good handful of petals or leaves, a tablespoon or so of seeds – and simmer for a minute or two. Leave to cool and infuse for at least 10 minutes before straining and using the milk or cream exactly as you normally would to create custard, ice cream and all.

Making a flavoured syrup (1) is very much the same idea, except what you end up with is a fairly complete thing: a sweet and clear syrup that carries within it a ghostly waft of your chosen ingredient. Simple syrup is a thing that is easiest done the American way, with ingredients measured out using cups rather than millilitres and grams, as you want roughly equal volumes of sugar and water (or a bit less sugar for a less dense syrup, down to a water: sugar ratio of 2:1). Warm them gently together in a saucepan, stirring, until the sugar dissolves, then bring to the boil and add your chosen ingredient, simmer for a few minutes then leave to cool completely (or longer, for stronger flavours). Pour the syrup through a muslin into sterilised jars and store in the fridge. You can then pour your fennel seed syrup over slices of blood oranges or your rosemary syrup over apple pancakes. You can also use syrups as the base of other recipes: make an oregano syrup and turn it into a sorbet, make a bay syrup and use it as the base of a wintry champagne cocktail.

Infusions in alcohol (2) are simpler and the flavour transfer is made possible by alcohol and time, rather than heat. Choose a high-proof spirit (vodka is good for its lack of competing flavours) and try adding whichever flavours take your fancy. You can do this in really quite small quantities, taking one bottle of vodka and filling several jars: one with tarragon, one with caraway seed, one with nasturtium flowers, and so on. Let them macerate for 10–15 days, shaking the jars daily, and then strain them off. You can immediately turn them into liqueurs by adding a simple syrup, or use them unsweetened: tarragon vodka with limoncello and soda water, caraway seed vodka with orange juice, nasturtium flower vodka in a peppery bloody Mary.

# Perennial herbs

The leaves of perennial herbs have the strength of flavour of those of the annual herbs, but are borne on plants that spring back into life every spring, with no need for fussy sowing. Some, such as rosemary, sage and bay, are evergreen, out there battling the weather all winter long, and as such their leaves are tough, although packed with flavour. Others die down in winter and return to life in spring, and these have leaves that are soft as well as flavourful, which you would happily pick and munch straight from the plant. And then there are the slightly tender perennial herbs that do need a little cosseting, but will reward your care with some of the finest flavours.

## Bay

One of the biggest and toughest of the herbs, bay trees can grow vast: almost as big as you will let them: once you have planted a bay tree you will never be short of leaves. Bay is oddly versatile for such a sturdy thing, and its leaves do both savoury and sweet. The flavours must be drawn out by slow simmering, though, and while in the early simmer they will release almost eucalyptus-like notes they soon mellow down to sweet and tea-like flavours. This is wonderful in a stock or a béchamel sauce, of course, but it's possibly even better in an ice cream.

## Scented geranium/pelargonium

The scented geranium flavour range is broad and bizarrely far-reaching. The underlying scent and taste is sharp, slightly lemony and green, a little minty and bitter, but from this starting point scented geraniums branch off in many different directions. The most common perhaps are the lemon-scented varieties, such as *Pelargonium* 'Citriodorum' and the rose-scented, such as *P.* 'Attar of Roses', but then there is 'Clorinda' (cedar), 'Prince of Orange' (orange), 'Ardwick Cinnamon' (cinnamon), 'Birdbush Bobby' (lime), 'Islington Peppermint' (peppermint), 'Old Spice' (spice) – even 'Cola Bottles Toronto' (cola). And I could go on – for quite some time! These are not leaves that you want to chop up and eat, but they are wonderful infused in milk or syrup, or for adding extra complexity to summery jams. Generally speaking the citrus- and rose-scented leaves are the best for cooking, but you could certainly experiment with the others. Perfumers often use geranium notes in rosy blends to extend and fill out rose notes, and to make them less sickly sweet and floral, and I think something similar to this happens flavour-wise when combining rose water with rose-scented geraniums, too.

Scented geraniums are not hardy and will be killed by frost. They can be brought indoors and treated as houseplants all winter – but ideally in a cool room or a porch, away from central heating – then returned to the outside in late spring and cut back hard (make use of those leaves) and encouraged to sprout new, fresh growth. Pick and use the leaves all summer long.

## Lemon verbena

This is one of the finest flavours in this book – and that's saying something. Lemon verbena is extraordinarily lovely: strongly lemony but sweet and sherbet-like. It makes the best possible tisane, and is worth growing even if that is all you ever do with it. Make it into a ridiculously summery syrup for dressing up fruit salads, pouring over ice cream or making into cocktails. I have also dried some of the leaves and then ground them up to make a sherbet, making the most of their already fizzy flavour.

The plant is not hugely hardy, but neither will it fare very well indoors all winter. If you have well-drained soil then plant it outside and take your chances. If not, keep it in a pot and place it in the most sheltered and sunny spot you have over winter, ideally a greenhouse. Keep it moist but not wet over winter and then chop it back hard once growth has started in spring.

## Mint

Mint is not just mint. There are many varieties, and while the prevailing taste of mint is pretty forthright and unambiguous, each has a subtle difference that lends it to a slightly different use.

The main difference is between spearmint, *Mentha spicata*, and peppermint, *Mentha × piperita*. Spearmint is the sweeter, spicier and gentler of the two, and it is the best one to use in combination with other herbs such as basil (as in a herb sugar) or with fruits. It is the flavour of chewing gum, but the group also contains the finest strain for making tea, Moroccan mint (*Mentha spicata* var. *crispa* 'Moroccan').

Peppermint is stronger and more strident, containing high levels of menthol, which stands up well to other flavours and has a cooling effect on the mouth – hence peppermint is the one to include in a fresh chutney to eat with hot food, or in a cooling raita. It is able to hold its own in savoury dishes with strong flavours, too. Notable varieties of peppermint include *Mentha* x *piperita* f. *citrata* 'Chocolate', with its distinct taste of After Eight mints.

*Mentha suaveolens*, apple mint, is soft-flavoured and has fruity notes. 'Pineapple' is one of its varieties, prettily variegated and with a scent of fresh pineapple. Both are very good chopped and sprinkled on a fruit salad.

Mints are almost too easy to grow. They thrive in damp and shade and have a (well-deserved) reputation as thugs in the garden. They need to be confined; either grown in pots in the usual manner or in a container sunk into garden soil. This will help keep them moist and happy, but prevent their roots ranging far and wide and smothering all other plants in their wake. They will die down in winter, but if you are on the case you can dig up a few roots in early autumn and pot them up. Kept on a windowsill indoors they will sprout and produce fresh winter leaves. Clumps of mint tend to die out from the middle and when grown in a pot plants can lose their vigour and start to look very sorry for themselves. Every couple of years, lift the plant and cut it up with a spade, discarding the dead central parts and planting up the lively bits from around the edges into new compost.

## Rosemary

The flowers of rosemary have appeared elsewhere in this book, but the leaf is a whole different kit and caboodle. More 'needle' in fact than 'leaf', rosemary falls decisively into the 'evergreen and tough with it' camp of perennial herbs. The flavour is beyond strong: vibrant and bracing, so much so that it is often just cooked close to other things – roasting potatoes and meats – this being enough to imbue them with its flavour. However, I wouldn't completely rule out eating it direct. Though I have most often just wafted it near food and considered that enough, I have come to really enjoy it chopped up very fine and included directly in breads and biscuits; the younger, softer summer leaves are maybe best for this, though I wouldn't discount using the needles in winter either, when herbs are scarce. It's an uncompromising flavour, but perhaps one that grows on you.

Being a Mediterranean silver-leaved herb, rosemary grows best on well-drained soil in full sun, though it is more of a survivor than many of the other Mediterranean herbs and I have seen it growing very vigorously on heavy clay soil, so it is always worth a go. Maybe plant in the spring to give it a head start in the summer months, rather than in autumn or winter.

111

## Tarragon

Strongly aniseed-flavoured tarragon dies down over winter and grows back from the ground in spring, so the leaves are always soft and relatively young. They can certainly be chopped and included directly in a dish. Tarragon is good in tomato sauces, egg dishes, stews, with fish and also goes famously well with chicken. It is widely used in French fine cooking and is one of their fines herbes, as well as being one of the main ingredients in buttery béarnaise sauce. It makes a brilliantly useful vinegar.

Take care to buy French tarragon (*Artemisia dracunculus*) and not Russian tarragon (*Artemisia dracunculoides*). Russian tarragon has a bitter note that is lacking in the sweeter French tarragon. Tarragon is not happy growing in pots as it has deep roots, so you need to plant it out in the garden.

# Tarragon oeufs en cocotte

This is such a simple little dish, but very elegant, and a perfect showcase for tarragon.

**Serves 4**

Butter, for greasing

150g crème fraîche

Sea salt and freshly ground black pepper

About 2 tablespoons finely chopped tarragon

4 large eggs

1. Preheat the oven to 180°C/gas mark 4.

2. Lightly butter 4 ramekins then put a spoonful of crème fraîche in the bottom of each with a pinch of salt and pepper and a sprinkling of tarragon. Crack an egg into each ramekin, then top with another spoonful of crème fraîche and another sprinkling of tarragon, salt and pepper. Place the ramekins into a deep baking dish and pour in enough hot water to come about halfway up their sides. Bake for about 15 minutes. Serve with toasted soldiers for dipping.

# Bay & semolina pudding with poached winter fruits & toasted hazelnuts

A delicately hued and fragranced dessert for a winter's night.

**Serves 4**

**For the poached fruits**

375ml white wine

375ml water

450g caster sugar

1 bay leaf

1 star anise

1 vanilla pod, split

2 quince

2 unripe pears

2 dessert apples

**For the bay semolina**

600ml full-fat milk

3 bay leaves

50g demerara sugar

65g semolina

80ml double cream

40g toasted and chopped hazelnuts, to serve

1. To make the poached fruit, put the wine, water, sugar, bay leaf, star anise and vanilla pod into a large saucepan and heat gently until the sugar dissolves. Peel, quarter and core the quinces, putting them straight into the poaching liquid so that they don't have time to discolour. Bring the poaching liquid up to a gentle simmer. The quinces will be cooked in a relatively short time - after 20 minutes or so they will be soft enough to eat – but if you can simmer them for longer you will be rewarded by a beautiful intensifying of colour and flavour. Simmer for a couple of hours and you will have ruby red poaching liquid and deep blush tinged pieces of fruit. The pears should be peeled, quartered and cored and added for the final 20 minutes of cooking, the apples (peeled, quartered, cored) for the final 5 minutes of cooking time. Spoon the fruit into a dish and set aside, then continue to simmer the syrup until it is further reduced, and thick and sticky, when it should be removed from the heat.

2. Put the milk and bay leaves into a saucepan and heat, slowly bringing it to the boil, then remove from the heat and leave to steep for 30 minutes. Warm the milk again until it gently simmers, then add the sugar and semolina, and stir for 12-15 minutes until the mixture thickens. Stir in half the double cream.

3. Serve the semolina pudding warm, with the poached fruits and a sprinkling of nuts, topped with quince syrup and the remainder of the double cream.

# Mint ice cream in a chocolate cookie sandwich

Making mint choc chip ice cream with fresh mint turns the mintiness right up. It is lovely to be able to properly taste the herb, and I both infuse the mint in the milk and add some fresh chopped mint during churning. Both peppermint and spearmint are great in this, but they do produce quite a different effect; the spearmint is gentler and more nuanced, the peppermint strident. Do use the chocolate peppermint *Mentha × piperita* f. *citrata* 'Chocolate', if you can get hold of it.

**Makes about 10 ice cream sandwiches**

**For the ice cream**

500ml full-fat milk

1 large bunch of mint, ½ left whole, ½ leaves finely chopped

6 egg yolks

125g caster sugar

150ml double cream

150g dark chocolate, chopped into little chunks

**For the chocolate cookies**

200g salted butter, softened

300g soft brown sugar

2 eggs

300g self-raising flour

80g cocoa powder

1 teaspoon baking powder

300g dark chocolate, chopped into chunks

1. Preheat the oven to 180°C/gas mark 4.

2. Put the milk and the whole mint sprigs into a saucepan and bring to the boil. Simmer gently for a minute or two and then leave to cool for 10 minutes before removing the mint.

3. In a large bowl, whisk together the egg yolks and sugar, then pour in a little of the warm milk, whisking all the time. Pour in the remainder of the milk and whisk briefly. Clean the pan and return the mixture to it. With the heat on low, stir the mixture continuously until it thickens (for tips on preventing curdling, see page 29). It is ready when the custard is thick enough to coat the back of a spoon and you can draw a clean line through it with your finger. Leave to cool, then chill for at least a couple of hours. Whisk the double cream to soft peaks and mix it into the chilled custard. Add the chocolate and the chopped mint leaves and churn in an ice-cream maker. When it has become thick and well churned, transfer it to a freezerproof container, cover with a lid and freeze for at least six hours or overnight.

4. To make the cookies, cream together the butter and sugar until fluffy, then beat in the eggs, one at a time. Sift in the flour, cocoa and baking powder and tip in the chocolate chunks. Fold together carefully until well combined. Line a baking tray with baking parchment and spoon tablespoons of the mixture onto it, spaced apart. You may need a couple of trays. Bake in the oven for about 16 minutes – the cookies should still be slightly soft when you take them out of the oven, but place them on a wire rack and they will harden as they cool.

5. Take the ice cream out of the freezer 20 minutes before you want to serve it, to allow it to soften. Sandwich 1–2 scoops between 2 cookies to serve.

# Rosemary, orange & chocolate biscotti

I shied away from putting rosemary into the fabric of recipes for years, until I tried it in a bread and loved its resinous herbiness. Perhaps it's an acquired taste, but I have absolutely acquired it, and combined with orange and chocolate I find it just delicious. You must serve these with a glass of syrupy vin santo to dip into.

**Makes 12–15**

110g plain flour, plus extra for dusting

1 teaspoon baking powder

Pinch of salt

25g ground almonds

75g caster sugar

2 tablespoons finely chopped rosemary

Grated zest of 2 oranges

75g dark chocolate, chopped into chunks

1 large egg, beaten

1. Preheat your oven to 160°C/gas mark 3.

2. Sift the flour, baking powder and salt into a large bowl, then add the ground almonds, sugar, rosemary, orange zest and chocolate chunks. Give it a stir and then add the egg and stir again to evenly combine, before going in with your hands and bringing it together into a dough.

3. On a lightly floured surface, make the dough into a log about 30cm long, place it on a baking tray covered with baking parchment and bake for 30 minutes. The log should still be pale in colour when you remove it. Let it cool down completely and, in the meantime, reduce the oven temperaure to 150°C/gas mark 2.

4. Slice the log into diagonal slices, place the discs on the tray, spaced apart, and bake for 30 minutes in the slightly cooler oven. Transfer the biscotti to a wire rack to cool completely.

# Sugars, sherbets & sprinkles

Sprinkles – the oldest trick in the book. Nothing jazzes up a dessert as effortlessly as a pretty and colourful flower-, herb- or seed-flavoured sugar. They turn cakes, ice creams and bowls of fruit into something really special: ta da! They are especially wonderful when used to frost the rim of a cocktail glass.

Perhaps the simplest are the floral sugars. With a strongly scented flower such as lavender, all you need to do is layer a couple of flowers in a jar of sugar and wait for a week or two (1). For quicker results, smash together – say – rose petals and sugar with a pestle and mortar and use straight away (3): the colour from the petals will bleed into the sugar, turning it pink, purple or yellow. Also try either method with jasmine, clove pinks, rosemary flowers, oregano flowers, chamomile, marigold and violet. Once you have made the floral sugar you can either use it as a finishing touch on poached peaches and cream, or include it in place of ordinary sugar when baking a summery Victoria sponge.

Turn seeds and nuts into a sprinkle by making a brittle and then smashing it up (2). You need to choose the seeds that lend themselves to sweet uses, such as fennel, sweet cicely, caraway, poppy, sunflower, pumpkin and all the nuts. When using the tiny seeds, use about 35g seeds and 25g caster sugar; for the nuts, use about 80g nuts and 30g sugar. Toast the seeds or nuts in a pan until golden, then add the sugar and stir it as it starts to melt. Once it has formed a runny, deep amber caramel, tip the lot out onto a baking tray lined with baking parchment or a silicone mat. With the tiny seeds you should then immediately place a second piece of parchment or a silicone mat on top and roll the brittle flat with a rolling pin. When the caramel has completely cooled, smash it into tiny pieces and sprinkle it over a chocolate banana sundae or a fig and honey ice cream.

Gremolata is a savoury combination of herbs, salt, lemon zest and sometimes garlic, but you can also make a sweet gremolata (4) using sugar instead of salt. Mint and basil are particularly well suited to this. Chop up a handful of leaves, finely pare a strip of lemon so that you take none of the white pith, and chop this up finely. Combine the lemon zest, herbs and a couple of tablespoons of sugar and then sprinkle this onto a lemon sorbet or a plate of strawberries.

Use dried petals, leaves and seeds to make flavoured sherbets (5). Combine ¼ teaspoon of citric acid, 1 teaspoon of bicarbonate of soda, 60g of sifted icing sugar and a teaspoon of your chosen dried and ground flavouring, here fennel seeds, to rim the edge of a glass of herb-infused martini.

# *Seed*

Fennel seed, lovage seed, sweet cicely seed, caraway seed, cumin seed, coriander seed, almond, hazelnut, walnut, mustard seed, radish seed, nasturtium seed, poppy seed, pumpkin seed, sunflower seed.

# Herb seeds

Many herbs have a second act; after the anticipated flush of greenery to chop onto salads and into sauces, along comes another crop, one carrying even more flavour. The seeds of herbs are such a bonus because they are often unexpected: the result of some slack gardening perhaps, or of failing to clear plants once the leaves are no longer useful. But these plants are worth actively cultivating for their seeds, or at least mindfully neglecting. In truth, all you have to do is fail to get around to pulling them up once the leaves are no longer tempting. These seeds really pack a punch: a whole potential plant is contained within each of them, along with a good proportion of its untapped flavour.

## Fennel

Fennel seeds are sweet and complex aniseed bombs. It's not only the seeds that you can eat, though; fennel is edible at all stages of its life, and this is one of the plants that gives you a ridiculously good payoff for growing your own. You can eat the young ferny fronds in spring and summer with fish or blended into a pesto; boil the stalks to make fragrant vegetable stock; slow-cook the flowers with pork in milk in the Italian style; or scatter the beautiful yellow pollen onto fruit salads. And then along come the seeds, which can be quite different depending on when you pick them. Just after flowering, freshly set and plump, they have a sweet greenness and make an excellent tisane. Try them at this stage mixed into salted yogurt as a dip, in coleslaw, or thrown in to slow-cook with buttery cabbage. As they dry they become nuttier and incredibly versatile, and are used in everything from naan breads to fish dishes, to charcuterie to sausage rolls, as well as in Indian and North African spice mixes. They are wonderful in sweet things, too, such as masala chai tea, biscotti, shortbread and fudge.

You will need to look for plants or seed of herb fennel, rather than Florence fennel, which is grown as an annual for its bulb-like swollen stems. Herb fennel is a perennial, so you will only plant it once but you will be able to harvest ferny leaves, flowers and seeds year after year.

## Lovage

Whenever I visited my Oma's for Sunday lunch as a child there was a bottle of Maggi sauce on the table. I loved its savoury, celery, strongly umami and almost meaty flavour, and I splashed it onto roast potatoes with abandon. As time went on it gradually fell out of favour and even my second-generation Dutch family cast it aside with mutterings about MSG and sodium levels, and the taste vanished from my life, unremarked. It was on getting hold of a handful of lovage seeds for the first time that those umami-spattered roasties came flooding back to me. The scent and flavour is wonderfully similar, so much so that in Germany and Holland (where the sauce is still, incidentally, much loved) it is known as 'Maggi herb'. The leaves of lovage are the part most often used, chopped up and added to soups, salads, with eggs or on potato salads, but the seeds are also wonderful, particularly crusted onto meat or baked veg, or baked into breads. It is often lovage seed that is used in celery salt, rather than celery seed itself.

Lovage is a hardy perennial, so you should only need to plant it once (in spring, after the frosts have passed, if only to give it the best possible start). Plant a few so that you can have one or two to chop back for leaf and another that you can allow to go to flower and seed.

## Sweet cicely

By some clever trick the anise in sweet cicely makes sweet things taste sweeter. It does great things for sharp, tart fruits such as rhubarb and gooseberry, and also allows you to cut back on the sugar used with other sweet things, while adding an aromatic waft of its very own. You can use every part – flowers, leaves and seeds – but it is the seeds that I have come to be particularly fond of. They are incredibly fleeting, eaten only when they are just formed and still green, and you can chop them up and sprinkle them onto baked fruits, include them in biscuits, or infuse them in custards and syrups. Sweet and anise with a gentle hint of liquorice, they really are something a little special, but as they dry the flavour ebbs away. You really have to grow your own and pick them fresh from the plant in midsummer if you want to capture this elusive flavour.

Luckily the growing is easy. This is a perennial herb, so it only needs to be sown once and it will come back year after year. Seed must be fresh, and it will not germinate without a period of cold. Either sow into pots in autumn and place the pots outside where they will be hit by frosts all winter, or put the seeds in a little damp compost in the fridge for a few weeks before sowing.

## Caraway

Caraway seeds have an earthy, slightly bitter liquorice flavour, with hints of citrus and aniseed. The plant also has edible, if bitter, leaves, but these are rarely eaten. Even the seed is one to use sparingly. Bake it in breads (particularly dark, uncompromising rye breads) and in sweet biscuits, where it is odd and almost jarring against the sweetness – one of those complicated and challenging tastes that wakes your tastebuds when used with blander, more comforting things. It likes cabbage, so scatter it into sauerkraut or coleslaw, and when frying cabbage in butter.

Caraway is a biennial: sow fresh seed in late summer and it will put on a little growth before winter, then the following summer it will flower and you will have seed in autumn. Harvest the whole seedheads before they turn brown and pop them into a paper bag to dry completely. After a few weeks the seeds will have dropped out into the bag. Pour the seeds into an airtight container and they are ready to use or to store.

## Cumin

Cumin is another edible herb that is primarily grown for its seeds, although the leaves are much used in Thai cooking. Warm, earthy and nutty with lemony notes, cumin seed is essential in Mexican, Latin American, Indian, south Asian and North African cuisines. Chilli con carnes and curries would be duller without it.

It is an annual but it does need a fairly long growing season so it should be sown under cover in autumn or indoors in early spring and planted out when the frosts have passed. Flowers will be produced in summer and seeds in late summer. Save the seeds just as you would caraway seeds.

## Coriander

I always used to curse coriander for going to flower so easily when I wanted it to produce big bunches of foliage. But that was before I started harvesting the unripe seed. Green coriander seed is a brilliant ingredient, soft and easy to bite into, its flavour is a cross between the citrusy, peppery and slightly soapy leaf and the warmer, nuttier, spicier dried seed. It can be eaten raw, just sprinkled over blander dhals or zingy Thai salads, over Asian seafood broths or blended up into a fresh chutney. Light cooking will make its flavour gentler, either baked into a naan bread or used as a last ingredient in a stir-fry.

Coriander loves to bolt, particularly towards midsummer, so you will have no problem getting your plants to produce seed. If you sow seed at the start of spring the plants are fairly likely to run to seed in summer, but only on puny plants. Better to sow in autumn and enjoy an autumn, winter and spring of leaves, before allowing these then-big plants to produce flower and seed the following summer. Harvest when green and use straight away, or if you want some to use as dried coriander then leave some to dry on the plant or cut off the browning heads and store them in paper bags until completely dry.

127

# Quails' eggs with dipping salt

Dip soft-boiled quails' eggs into moreish dipping salt. You can also use this flavoured salt like dukkah: dip bread into olive oil and then into the salt, then eat. You can make this more of a spread by whipping up a couple of other dipping salts (see page 140), and maybe an aioli and a pesto for dipping, too.

**Serves 2, as a starter**

6 quails' eggs

1 tablespoon cumin seeds

1 tablespoon dried thyme

1 tablespoon flaky sea salt

1. Cook the quails' eggs in a pan of boiling water for 2½ minutes, then drain and run under cold water to stop them cooking.

2. While the eggs are cooking, crush together the cumin seeds, thyme and half the salt with a pestle and mortar. Add the other half of the salt (you want to keep some nice big flakes) and mix together gently.

3. Once the eggs are cool enough to handle, peel them and serve alongside the dipping salt.

# Green coriander seed chutney with onion seed puris

In India a chutney is more often a blend of fresh ingredients, maybe made piquant with a little lemon juice, and eaten within a few days, rather than the more familiar Anglo-Indian chutney which is a long-lasting preserve heavy with sugar and vinegar. This fresh and light green coriander seed chutney comprises little other than coriander and green coriander seeds. If you have more coriander seeds – and they are produced in bulk on good-sized plants – change the ratio so there are more of them and less of the leaf. Puris are traditionally served with a potato curry and chutneys. Try some contrasting flavours, such as a sweet date and tamarind chutney and a yogurt and cucumber raita.

**Makes 1 small bowl chutney and 8 small puris**

The leaves from 1 big bunch of coriander (about enough to fill a 250ml jug)

4 tablespoons green coriander seeds

1 green chilli, deseeded and roughly chopped

1 teaspoon finely grated fresh ginger

Juice of ½ lemon

Salt

**For the puris**

120g plain flour

1 tablespoon onion seeds

½ teaspoon salt

Approximately 120ml water

Vegetable or sunflower oil, for deep-frying

1. Put all of the coriander leaves, half the coriander seeds, the chilli, ginger and lemon juice into a small blender and blend together briefly (or chop the leaf and mash it all together with a pestle and mortar: the results will be chunkier but still very good). Mix the last few whole coriander seeds into the chutney, along with a pinch of salt.

2. For the puris, in a bowl, mix the flour, onion seeds and salt, then add the water, a little at a time, mixing with your fingers until you have a fairly stiff dough. You may need a little less or a little more water; judge as you go. Knead the dough for several minutes, then divide it into eight pieces and roll each into a ball and coat lightly in oil – the oil will stop the dough sticking as you roll each out into a flat circle, not too thin, perhaps a little under 2mm in thickness.

3. Cover the dough circles with a tea towel to prevent them drying out and heat the oil in a large, deep saucepan or wok to 190°C, or until a piece of dough quickly starts bubbling and rises immediately to the surface when dropped in. Put one puri at a time into the pan and ladle hot oil over the top as it rises to the surface. Once it has puffed up, carefully flip it over and cook it on the other side for a minute. If it doesn't puff up, the oil isn't hot enough. Once both sides are golden and toasty, use a slotted spoon to lift the puri from the oil and drain it on kitchen paper. Eat while hot with a dollop of chutney.

# Dukkah-crusted lamb rack with pomegranate molasses

Dukkah is an Egyptian condiment made from crushed toasted hazelnuts, coriander seeds, cumin seeds, sesame seeds and salt and pepper. You can make your own or buy it ready made, and either way it makes a handsome, nutty and aromatic crust to a lamb rack.

**Serves 2**

4-bone lamb rack

3 tablespoons pomegranate molasses, plus more for drizzling

5 tablespoons dukkah

1. Remove the rack of lamb from the fridge 20 minutes before cooking to bring it up to room temperature.

2. Preheat your oven to 190°C/gas mark 5.

3. Place the rack of lamb on a baking tray, fat-side up, and coat with the pomegranate molasses using a pastry brush to ensure all the meat is well covered. Then sprinkle over the dukkah. Roast for 25–30 minutes for rare, 35 minutes for medium-rare or 40 minutes for well done. Remove from the oven and rest for 5 minutes before slicing between the bones with a sharp knife. Serve two chops per person.

# Apple fritters with fennel sugar

Apple is one of the many sweet things that fennel complements, particularly when ground up into a fragrant sugar. Apples are moist and can release moisture as they cook, making the batter soggy, so do take the time to dry them off carefully pre-battering.

**Serves 4**

**For the fennel sugar**

1 tablespoon dried fennel seeds

2 tablespoons granulated sugar

**For the apple fritters**

4 apples, cored and sliced into rings then tossed in lemon juice

200g plain flour

65g caster sugar

1 teaspoon dried fennel seeds

2 eggs

2 tablespoons salted butter, melted

Vegetable oil, for deep-frying

Honey, to serve

1. To make the fennel sugar, grind up the seeds with a pestle and mortar, add the sugar and grind both together.

2. Pat the apple rings dry with kitchen paper and then lay them out on a double layer of kitchen paper, with another layer covering them. Press the paper down onto the rings and leave for 5 minutes.

3. Fill a heavy-bottomed saucepan one-third full with oil and heat to 180°C. Mix the flour, sugar and fennel seeds together in a bowl and drop in the apple rings, turning them until they are all coated. Beat the eggs and melted butter together in a separate bowl and pour it over the floured apple rings. Mix until the rings are roughly coated in the thick gluey batter, then fry, a couple at a time, for a few minutes on each side, until they are golden and crispy. Remove with a slotted spoon and drain on kitchen paper.

4. Eat the fritters while hot, drizzled with honey and sprinkled with fennel sugar.

# Gooseberry & sweet cicely shortbreads

Fresh green sweet cicely seeds add perfect little nubs of aniseed to the shortbread and when scattered over gooseberries. You can, of course, stew the gooseberries, but I like baking them to concentrate the flavour and lightly caramelise the skins.

**Serves 6**

**For the shortbreads**

150g soft salted butter

70g golden caster sugar, plus 2 tablespoons for sprinkling

150g plain flour, plus extra for dusting

70g rice flour

2 tablespoons green sweet cicely seeds, roughly chopped

Pinch of salt

**For the baked gooseberries**

400g gooseberries, topped and tailed

2 tablespoons runny honey

**To serve**

275g Greek yogurt

1 tablespoon green sweet cicely seeds

1. Cream together the butter and sugar until light and fluffy, then add the flours, sweet cicely seeds and salt. Mix together roughly, then use your hands to bring the mixture into a dough. Roll out onto a floured surface, cut into rounds and place these on a baking sheet covered in baking paper. Chill the shortbread for at least 30 minutes.

2. Preheat your oven to 180°C/gas mark 4. Remove the shortbread from the fridge and sprinkle over 2 tablespoons of caster sugar, then bake for 20–25 minutes. The shortbread should be the colour of pale straw. Cool on a wire rack.

3. Meanwhile, put the gooseberries into a baking tray and drizzle with honey. Bake at the same temperature for 20–30 minutes, or until some of the gooseberries have browned. Remove from the oven and leave to cool.

4. Place a shortbread on each plate and top with a spoonful or two of Greek yogurt, a spoonful or two of the gooseberries and their juices and a scattering of sweet cicely seeds.

# Aquavit-ish

This traditional Scandinavian spirit is almost entirely flavoured with seeds that you can grow yourself. It is bitter, complex and satisfying and is served chilled in small glasses, as an accompaniment to dark beer.

**Makes 1 litre**

1 litre vodka (40% proof)

2 tablespoons dried caraway seeds

1 tablespoon dried fennel seeds

1 tablespoon dried coriander seeds

1 pared strip of lemon zest, with no white pith

Put all of the ingredients into a sterilised glass jar with a seal. After a couple of days, remove the lemon zest. Leave the remaining ingredients to infuse for two weeks, shaking the jar every few days. Strain into four 225ml sterilised bottles and seal. Chill before serving with a glass of dark beer.

# Spiced hot chocolate

The mix of seeds and spices is inspired by those in garam masala, the Indian spice mix used in ayurvedic medicine for its warming qualities.

**Serves 2**

450ml full-fat milk

½ teaspoon dried cumin seeds

½ teaspoon dried coriander seeds

½ teaspoon dried fennel seeds

1 cinnamon stick

Seeds from 2 cardamom pods

1 bay leaf

2 cloves

A few black peppercorns

70g dark chocolate, grated

35g milk chocolate, grated

75ml single cream

Pinch of salt

1. Pour 300ml of the milk into a saucepan and add all the spices. Bring just to the boil then remove from the heat and leave to steep for 10 minutes. Strain off the spices, return the milk to the saucepan and warm it to near boiling again.

2. In a separate saucepan, heat the remaining 150ml milk to a boil and add both the chocolates, whisking continuously until they have melted completely. Pour on the spiced milk, add the cream and a pinch of salt and whisk to combine everything well. Serve hot.

# Salts, rubs & condiments

Combine garden herbs, seeds and even petals with salt or with each other and you create the savoury equivalent of the sugary sprinkle: little highlights of intense savoury flavours. Celery salt (1) is one of the simplest to make but is also especially versatile: a combination of either celery seeds or lovage seeds ground up with salt that can be sprinkled onto soups, mixed into cream cheese as a topping for baked potatoes, added to coleslaw, scattered over pork skin when making crackling, or dropped into a bloody Mary. The effect is straightforwardly savoury and lip smacking.

Za-atar (2) is a Middle-Eastern, herb-based condiment, primarily composed of dried oregano and sesame seeds but also mixed with dried marjoram and a little ground cumin and salt. To make your own, toast some sesame seeds until they are light brown, grind some dried oregano until fine and mix together. Dip bread into good extra virgin olive oil and then into za-atar; moisten a little za-atar with olive oil and spread it on dough before baking to make *manakeesh bi za-atar*; scatter it onto labneh or hummus; or rub it onto chicken or vegetables before roasting.

Dukkah (4) is an Egyptian (and nutty and seedy) equivalent made from hazelnuts, sesame seeds, coriander seeds, cumin seeds and salt, all toasted and roughly ground together. It makes a brilliant crust for meat, fish or vegetables, applied before roasting, and can also be used in many of the same ways as za-atar, but for a less herbal and more crunchy, nutty result.

Petals get in on this particular act by way of Moroccan ras el hanout (3) – more of a spice mix than a condiment, but often used in the way of dukkah and za-atar as a rub to infuse foods with its warm, pungent and sweet flavours. It is also stirred into rice, and is one of the ingredients that gives a tagine its subtle sweetness. A great many spices go into ras el hanout, and the recipe changes from maker to maker (not to mention the regional variations), but ground dried rose petals are among the most important ingredients, with dried lavender often added, too.

Gremolata (5) is an Italian condiment made by chopping fresh herbs with lemon zest and garlic. It is lively, herbal and zesty, and the perfect topping for a mellower, slow-cooked dish, such as the Italian braised veal shank dish, *osso buco alla Milanese*, which it traditionally accompanies. Chop a handful of parsley, a couple of strips of lemon zest (no pith) and some young, fresh garlic, combine and sprinkle. Also try substituting other soft herbs and other citrus flavours, or adding a few salt flakes or a little smoked salt: orange zest and mint; lime and coriander. Sprinkle these onto slow-cooked meat just before serving, over omelettes and onto steamed, buttery asparagus. Wherever a brightener is needed, apply gremolata.

# Nuts

Nuts are among the most physically present of the ingredients in this book: solid and filling rather than having a purely ephemeral flavour. Grow your own or go out foraging local trees and you can pick and eat them young, fresh and moist, or wait until they are mature, dried and strong in flavour.

## Almond

If you grow your own almonds you will have the very special pleasure of picking a few 'green'. Around midsummer your almonds will have soft, fuzzy green skins, at which point you can pluck a few from the tree and prise them open with a sturdy knife: inside you will find a little almond coated in a rubbery skin. Peel this back and pop the part-formed almond into your mouth. It will be silky, sweet and gently almondy. If you have a few, eat them sprinkled onto stewed plums or with a peach compote and Greek yogurt, or pop them into homemade apricot jam. As the almonds get older they become stronger in flavour and more solid and nutty.

Almonds hail from sunny Mediterranean climates and so need a warm spot with a well-drained soil. Wet roots will kill an almond tree dead. They flower very early in the year and if their blossom is hit by frost then you will have lost the crop for that year, so plant in your sunniest and most sheltered spot and avoid frost pockets. While your tree is small you can watch the weather forecast and keep a sheet of horticultural fleece handy to throw over it on cool nights, but this quickly becomes impractical as they grow. 'Robijn' and 'Ingrid' are the most reliable varieties for cooler climates. Take care not to plant an almond near to a peach tree as they can cross-pollinate, which will make the almonds bitter.

## Hazelnut

Harvesting hazelnuts is a game of hide and seek. You can only see the clusters of nuts from below, so to start the picking you must get inside, under the canopy, and look up. At first there is nothing, and you tell yourself that it must be a duff year, and then you spot one cluster, then another, then three more. Hazelnuts reveal themselves to the patient: you have to get your eye in. This is less pertinent once they have matured and you can scrabble about on the floor where they have fallen, but you will want to harvest some in late summer and early autumn when they are young, fresh, vegetable-like and crunchy and before the shell has fully hardened. Use them in salads or just as a snack. Later on they will harden and mature and can be stored for cracking by the fire at Christmas, toasting and chopping over warm salads of winter squash and bacon, or combining with chocolate every possible way.

Hazelnuts are woodland plants and so easy to grow in cooler, damper climates. They will cope with a little shade, too. Plant two or more compatible varieties and you will get better pollination and high yields. 'Kentish Cob' is an old variety with excellent flavour, 'Merveille de Bollwiller' (sometimes sold as 'Hall's Giant') is vigorous with large nuts, and 'Butler' is a heavy cropper. The three varieties are compatible.

### Walnut

Walnuts left alone will grow into big trees, far too big for the average garden, but with pruning you can keep them much smaller, up to about 3.5–4.5 metres in height. Look for one of the smaller varieties such as 'Rita'. Cut back new branches to six leaves and repeat this all summer long and it will stay relatively compact. Like almonds and hazelnuts, there is loveliness in the young, unripe walnut, and this is something you are unlikely to get hold of easily unless you grow your own or forage. Pick them green in late June, when first on your recipe list should be two shades of *nocino* – a sticky, walnut liqueur made in northern Italy. To make your own version, chop up about 25 walnuts and drop them into a litre of vodka along with 500g sugar, a cinnamon stick, a split vanilla pod and the zest of one lemon, seal up the bottle and shake it every few days for about three months, by which time the vodka will have turned deepest brown, with a treacly texture. As you siphon it off into small bottles for storage you can start a second batch with the same nuts, which will be paler and more delicate. Leave the walnuts to mature and turn hard on the tree and they become incredibly versatile: bake them into breads and sprinkle them onto thick pumpkin soups or over wintry salads of goat's cheese and beetroot; grind them to make the bases of thick, rich sauces and dips; caramelise them and eat them as sweet snacks or mix into carrot or coffee cakes.

# Young hazelnut & apple warm salad

Young hazelnuts picked in early autumn before they are hardened and nutty are crisp and almost vegetable-like.

**Serves 2**

A couple of handfuls of watercress

50g strips of pancetta

2 small apples, cored and quartered

50g Stilton

30g shelled green hazelnuts

1 teaspoon hazelnut oil

1 teaspoon runny honey

Sea salt and freshly ground black pepper

1. Wash and dry the watercress and arrange on two plates. In a hot pan, fry the pancetta until crispy, lift out and drain on kitchen paper. Put the apple pieces into the hot pancetta oil and fry until they just take on a little colour but are still crispy. Remove from the pan, arrange over the watercress, then divide up the pancetta and the Stilton and sprinkle them over, too.

2. Finally, add the hazelnuts, a little hazelnut oil, a little runny honey, a sprinkle of salt and a grind of pepper over each, before serving with good bread.

# Mauresque cocktail

A long, refreshing, almond-and-anise-tinted drink.

**Makes syrup for 8 mauresques**

**For the orgeat syrup**

200ml unsweetened almond milk

8 tablespoons caster sugar

8 drops almond extract

¼ teaspoon orange blossom water

**For the Mauresque**

1 shot pastis

Chilled water and ice cubes

1. To make the orgeat syrup, combine all of the ingredients in a jug and stir until the sugar has dissolved. Taste and add more orange blossom water if needed (they do vary in strength) or almond extract.

2. To make the Mauresque, pour one shot each of the orgeat syrup and pastis into a glass and top up with chilled water and ice cubes and give it a good stir.

# Roasted cod with muhammara, caramelised onions & toasted walnuts

Muhammara is a spicy dip originally from Aleppo, Syria, which until not so long ago was home to a vast pepper-growing and drying industry. This is one of the many sauces from around the world that is thickened with nuts, this time walnuts, though you can substitute with others to create different effects. Use muhammara as a dip or, as here, slavered onto fish and baked: the strongly flavoured sauce with the mild, white fish is gorgeous.

**Serves 2**

2 cod fillets (approx 180g each)

Vegetable oil, for frying

1 onion, halved and thinly sliced

25g walnuts, toasted and chopped

**For the muhammara**

3 red peppers

3 tablespoons extra virgin olive oil, plus extra for finishing

75g walnuts, toasted

50g breadcrumbs

1 garlic clove, peeled

A pinch of chilli flakes

1 tablespoon pomegranate molasses

1. First make the muhammara. Put the red peppers under a hot grill and cook them until they are completely blackened on one side, then turn, with tongs, and repeat until all sides are blackened. Pop them into a large bowl, cover with clingfilm and leave to cool. The clingfilm traps steam, which helps to separate the skin from the flesh.

2. When they are cool, pull off the blackened skin and discard the seedy inner, leaving just the flesh. Put the pepper flesh with all of the other muhammara ingredients into a food-processor and pulse until they are roughly combined, or pound with a pestle and mortar for a good rough texture (if you are making it by hand this way you will need to start with the garlic and nuts and slowly work in the other ingredients).

3. Preheat your oven to 200°C/gas mark 6. Lay the cod fillets on a baking tray and spoon a few tablespoons of muhammara onto each. Top with a little olive oil and then bake for 10–15 minutes until the fish is opaque and flakes easily.

4. Meanwhile, heat a little oil in a frying pan and fry the sliced onions until they turn brown and caramelised. They will not turn crispy until you lift them out of the oil and leave them to cool a little on kitchen paper.

5. Top the fish with the crispy onions and chopped walnuts and serve with a salad.

147

# Blackberry & hazelnut frangipane

Frangipane is normally made with almonds, a sort of semi-solid filling particularly well suited for pairing with apricots and plums and other stone fruit, but it can be made with any other nut just as successfully. I think hazelnuts and blackberries rub along just as happily in the kitchen as they do in the hedgerow.

Serves 8–10

**For the pastry**

110g cold salted butter, diced

225g plain flour, plus extra for dusting

110g caster sugar

3 egg yolks

**For the filling**

125g salted butter, softened

125g caster sugar

2 eggs

125g ground blanched hazelnuts

1 tablespoon plain flour

150g blackberries

A handful of blanched and roughly chopped hazelnuts

1. To make the pastry case, rub the cold butter into the flour and sugar until the mixture resembles breadcrumbs (or whizz them together in a food-processor). Add the egg yolks and bring everything together into a dough, then wrap in clingfilm and chill for 30 minutes.

2  Preheat the oven to 170°C/gas mark 4. Roll out the pastry on a flour-dusted surface and use to line a 23 x 2.5cm loose-bottomed tart tin, trimming the edges of the pastry so that they are flush with the top. Chill again while you prepare the frangipane.

3. Cream together the butter and the sugar until it is light and fluffy, then add the eggs, beating until each is combined before adding the next. Fold in the hazelnuts and flour and mix until well combined. Spread the frangipane evenly across the pastry base and then stud the surface with the blackberries and the chopped hazelnuts. Bake for 1 hour 10 minutes, or until the filling has risen up and turned toasty brown. Allow the tart to cool a little before serving.

# Almond, rose & cinnamon drop scones

It was on reading *The Miniaturist* by Jessie Burton that I first started craving the combination of almonds, rosewater, cardamom and cinnamon. Set in a merchant-packed and spice-filled seventeenth-century Amsterdam, these scents waft through the book, most particularly in the form of *oliekoeken*: little rose-, cardamom- and cinnamon-scented almond flour doughnuts. I have not made real *oliekoeken* (they turn out to be a faff of yeast and proving and deep-frying), but I have instead taken to mixing almond flour and a little rosewater and cinnamon into our weekend morning drop scones.

**Serves 4**

100g ground almonds

100g plain flour

15g caster sugar

2 teaspoons baking powder

1 teaspoon ground cinnamon

Seeds of 3 cardamom pods, ground

Pinch of salt

2 eggs

200ml full-fat milk

½ teaspoon rosewater

A little butter, for frying and dotting

**To serve**

Double cream

Honey

A handful of toasted, slivered almonds

A few rose petals

1. Preheat your oven to 150°C/gas mark 2 and place a large ovenproof dish into it to heat.

2. In a large bowl, mix together the ground almonds, plain flour, sugar, baking powder, cinnamon, cardamom and salt. Make a well in the centre, crack in the eggs and pour in a little of the milk. Whisk in small movements to start mixing in small amounts of the dry ingredients from the edges of the well. As the wet mix thickens, add more milk. Continue to whisk in small circles, and to add milk, until all the milk, rosewater and dry ingredients are combined, hopefully without too many lumps. The mixture should be thick: more like porridge than traditional pancake batter.

3. Melt a little butter into a frying pan over a medium heat and then ladle in three small dollops of batter. After a couple of minutes bubbles will appear all over the surface, flip over the little scones and cook for another minute or so, or until the bottom is crispy and browned. Lift the drop scones into the heated ovenproof dish and keep in the oven while you continue making scones until all of the mixture is used up.

4. Serve in a big, communal pile, dotted with melting butter and with plenty of cream poured over, plus honey, a scattering of almond slivers and rose petals.

# Sauces, frangipanes & soups

There is a worldwide tradition of using ground nuts as thickeners and bases, and it makes for some delicious sauces and soups.

Some delicious Mediterranean nut-thickened dips include romesco (3), which comprises red pepper, almonds, bread, garlic and oil; muhammara, with red pepper, walnuts and pomegranate molasses, which is also delicious made with beetroot instead of peppers (1); skordalia, made up of ground walnuts with garlic, potato and olive oil; tarator, which consists of walnuts, garlic, yogurt, lemon and herbs. Use nuts to thicken other vegetable sauces: beetroot muhammara is wonderful, as is roast winter squash blended with toasted walnuts, olive oil and garlic. Further afield there is peanut-based gado gado and satay, and almond-based korma (2), the nuts in each providing the bulk of the sauce and the mild backdrop against which the spices work.

The best known of the nut soups is ajoblanco, the Spanish almond and garlic chilled soup, but you can thicken soups with any nut – just grind them up fine and cook them long: try roast tomato and toasted cashew soup, and roasted cauliflower and hazelnut soup.

Grind up any nuts and combine them with butter, eggs and sugar to make frangipane, a nutting filling for tarts, and beautiful topped with fruit before baking (see page 149).

# Vegetable & flower seeds

Once your flowers have been admired all summer long, your vegetables have been plucked and all is starting to fade away ready for clearing, hold your hand. Don't grub up flower borders and vegetable patches until you have scoured them for the precious edible seeds that some leave behind. This is a motley, varied and useful crew; some big, oily and nutty, others tiny and strongly peppery or piquant. This late bounty is a prize for the not-too-tidy gardener.

### Mustard

Mustard seed is a real coup, very much a spice-cupboard regular, but very easy to gather from spent plants of the oriental mustard leaves. When dried and ground up, mustard is of course fiery and nose-popping, but when dry-fried or fried in oil as part of a temper for curries, it takes on more of a nutty flavour. I gather seeds from the Oriental mustards. I generally sow these in late summer for winter leaves and find that the plants go to seed the following spring. Those sown in spring will often flower and set seed in summer. You can use the seeds unripe, when they are a little less hot and a little fresher, or let them dry on the plant and then collect them up. When dry, the seedheads can rather explode, spraying the seeds around, so cover the seedheads with a paper bag and then try to break them off, whole. Leave the whole seedhead in the bag for a couple of days, by which time the seeds and seedheads will have parted company and you can pour them into a jar for storage without drama.

### Radish

Fail to harvest a radish and it will send up a flower spike which will soon be covered in reams of fat, juicy, green seed pods, all with the same pepperiness of the original radish, only milder, as long as you pick them young. It makes you wonder why anyone ever picks the actual radish, so abundant does the plant become if you neglect it. Scatter these pods over salads, put them in sandwiches for crunch, pickle them or just throw them straight into stir-fries.

If you want to grow specifically for seed pods, go for radish 'Rat's Tail', which is particularly prolific in thin, tender seed pods, but really any old radish will produce them too, and you can sow a row and harvest a few of the swollen roots, before leaving the rest to go to seed. They are very easy to grow: sow direct into the soil any time from spring to autumn.

### Nasturtium

Nasturtiums do everything: they have edible flowers, leaves and seeds, are good-looking all summer long, and are enthusiastic self-seeders, so you don't even have to remember to sow them once you've got them going. There really is every excuse to grow them. The flowers popped up earlier in this book, but I want to give a special mention to the seeds. Rustle around in the undergrowth of a nasturtium planting from late summer onwards and you will come across the clusters of seeds where the flowers have fallen away. You need to pick them young and green, while they still cling to each other in trios – once they have grown so big that they push apart they are almost inedibly harsh and hot, but when young they are peppery and crunchy and very lovely indeed. You can scatter them on salads as they come, or pickle them, which seems to suit their peppery nature. Once pickled, use them much as you would capers: in caponata, in pasta sauces and vinaigrettes, in potato salads and with grilled fish.

### Poppy

The seeds of the opium poppy, *Papaver somniferum*, are produced abundantly, as anyone who has ever tried to eradicate them from a garden or allotment will attest. Just one stray seedhead, left until it has dried into a little round pepperpot, and a whole new generation of poppies will be born. This makes the poppy a very easy plant to keep going, and if you are really sick of them you can pull up the silvery green seedlings in spring. Sprinkle the dried seeds onto the surface of bread before baking, for a beautiful and nutty finish, or grind them into poppy seed butter for filling cakes and pastries.

Sow seeds in spring – you will only have to do so the once – and harvest carefully once the seedhead has started to dry out. Once they are fully dry they should store well, so collect plenty for a year's worth of seedy breads.

### Pumpkin

This is one of the meatier and more substantial of the seeds, verging on nut-like. They are absolutely at their best lightly toasted until the skins crack, making the seed jump in the pan, but you can also sprout them by soaking them in water for 12 hours then draining and storing them in an open-topped jar or sprouter. You will then need to 'wash' and drain them every 12 hours for a few days, after which they will be bursting with enzymes, vitamins and bio-available bits and pieces. The problem for the grower of pumpkins (and indeed winter squash) is getting the seeds out of their shells. If you want to make use of those that are within the winter squash and pumpkins you are growing for flesh you have a bit of a palaver on your hands, though not an insurmountable one. First wash the seeds, then toast them lightly, to separate seed from hull. Let them cool and then tip them into a plastic bag and roll over the bag lightly with a rolling pin. Next, pour all of the broken seeds into a large bowl of water and agitate to separate:

the husks will float on the top and the seeds will sink to the bottom. But you can also choose to grow 'naked seed' varieties, which have very soft, edible shells. The flesh isn't great, so you will be growing these for seed. Choose from 'Lady Godiva' and 'Baby Bear'.

Sow pumpkins and winter squash seeds indoors in early spring and plant out in a sunny spot into soil that has been enriched with well-rotted manure in late spring or early summer, when the frosts have passed. Harvest pumpkins and winter squash before the first frosts.

## Sunflower

Sunflower seeds have many of the same qualities and problems as pumpkin seeds. They are bulky and oily, tastiest when toasted and healthiest when sprouted, but there are the same problems with accessing the seed. If you want to just sit and eat them as a snack then do toast a few with salt and sit and crack them with your teeth, but if you want to harvest them in bulk you will have to try the toasting, rolling and floating method outlined for pumpkin seeds. Unfortunately there are no naked seeded varieties, however the tallest sunflowers – 'Russian Giant', 'Mongolian Giant', 'Giant Single' – will produce the biggest seeds. Sow sunflowers in early spring indoors and plant outside once the frosts have passed.

# Seeded water biscuits with marinated feta

Homemade savoury crackers are incredibly quick and straightforward to make, and so many notches above shop-bought versions. I like to make one big sheet and crack it apart into shards once baked, but you can cut the sheet into little squares before baking if you prefer a neater cracker. This is a wonderful way to show off your home-harvested seeds. Use whatever you have to hand, but use plenty of fennel seeds in among the milder seeds.

Serves 6

**For the marinated feta**

200g feta cheese

Extra virgin olive oil

2 teaspoons chipotle chilli flakes

1 smoked garlic clove (unsmoked if you can't find it), thinly sliced

**For the biscuits**

200g plain flour

½ teaspoon baking powder

1 teaspoon salt

50g cold salted butter, cut into cubes

4 tablespoons water

4 tablespoons each of sunflower, pumpkin and fennel seeds

1 tablespoon sea salt flakes

1. Marinate the feta the night or a few hours before you want to eat it. Put it in a small bowl, pour over olive oil to cover and sprinkle on the chilli flakes and garlic. Cover with clingfilm and set aside.

2. Preheat your oven to 180°C/gas mark 4.

3. To make the biscuits, mix together the flour, baking powder and salt in a large bowl then rub in the butter until the mixture resembles fine breadcrumbs. Pour in the water and bring together into a dough, adding a little more water if necessary. Knead briefly, then roll out into a rectangle and trim the edges to fit your largest baking tray. Cover that baking tray with a piece of baking paper, lay the rolled out dough onto it, and then brush with water and scatter on the seeds, evenly across the entire surface or in ribbons. Press them down lightly all over and then scatter over the salt flakes. Bake for 10–15 minutes or until golden and toasty. Remove and leave to cool.

4. Once cool, break the biscuits into shards and eat with the feta.

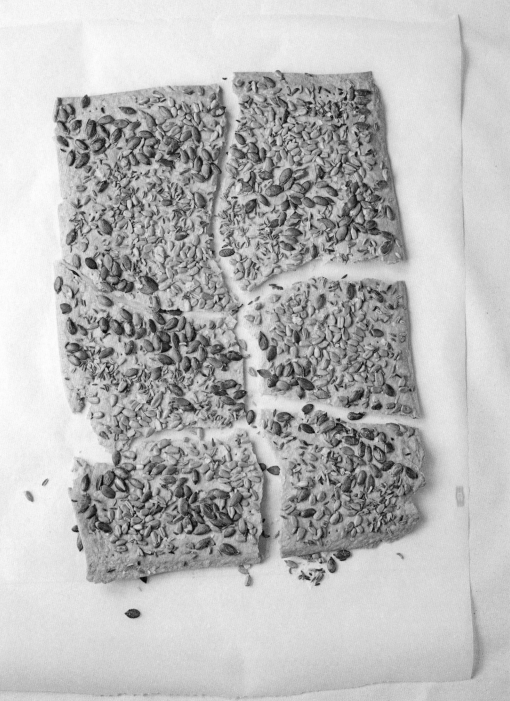

# Radish seed pakora

This is a brilliant way to make use of a glut of peppery radish seeds.

**Makes 12–15 pakoras**

Vegetable or sunflower oil, for deep-frying

50g gram flour

2 teaspoons garam masala

1 teaspoon ground turmeric

1 teaspoon cumin seeds

½ teaspoon chilli flakes

1 teaspoon salt

200g radish seeds

A handful of chopped coriander leaves

Lemon wedges, to serve

**For the minted yogurt**

A handful of chopped mint

Pinch of salt

4 tablespoons Greek yogurt

1. Fill a saucepan one-third full with oil and start to heat it. Put the gram flour, dry spices and salt in a bowl, stir briefly, then drop in the radish seeds and chopped coriander and mix. Stir in a little water, adding just enough that the flour turns into a thick and sticky coating for the seed pods. Start to fry when the oil reaches 180°C or when a small piece of batter dropped in starts to bubble immediately and quickly rises to the surface.

2. Scoop spoonfuls of the batter and lower them into the oil, perhaps three at a time. Let them fry for several minutes on one side, until crispy and brown, then flip them over and cook on the other side for another few minutes. Lift out with a slotted spoon and drain on kitchen paper.

3. Mix the mint and salt into the yogurt and serve with the hot pakoras and some lemon wedges.

# Warm potato, egg & pickled nasturtium salad

This is a great place to use nasturtium seeds: they add a crunchy, sharp and peppery flavour against the blandness of the warm potato. The pickled seeds will keep for months, but once the jar is opened, keep it in the fridge and use the seeds within a few weeks.

**Serves 4**

**For the pickled nasturtium seeds**

100g young nasturtium seeds

75ml white wine vinegar

75ml water

3 tablespoons granulated sugar

1½ teaspoons salt

Pinch of lovage seeds

A few peppercorns

**For the potato salad**

1kg waxy potatoes, cut into large pieces

4 eggs

2 tablespoons pickled nasturtium seeds

1 shallot, finely diced

1 large bunch of lovage or parsley

Juice of 1 lemon

8 tablespoons extra virgin olive oil

1 teaspoon Dijon mustard

Sea salt and freshly ground black pepper

1. To pickle the nasturtium seeds, first pack them into a sterilised 150ml jar. Gently heat all of the other ingredients together in a small saucepan until the sugar dissolves, then bring it to a simmer and pour it over the seeds. Seal the jar while the ingredients are still hot, then leave to cool. The pickled nasturtium seeds will be ready to eat after a day or two but their flavour will improve if they are left for longer.

2. To make the salad, cook the potatoes in a pan of boiling water for about 15 minutes or until tender, then drain and put into a large bowl. Cook the eggs in a pan of boiling water for 7 minutes, cool them in cold water, then peel, roughly chop and add them to the bowl along with the nasturtium seeds and the shallot. Pull the leaves off the lovage or parsley stems, chop them finely and add them to the bowl.

3. Put the lemon juice, olive oil, Dijon mustard, salt and pepper into a jar and shake to combine, then pour this dressing over the salad and gently turn the salad until everything is coated.

# Pumpkin soup with pistou & toasted pumpkin seeds

I love a good soup and topping combination, so here it is: sweet creamy soup, herby pistou and crunchy seeds. I have called this pumpkin soup for seed symmetry but I actually use winter squash over pumpkin every time. The flesh is sweeter, denser and far more flavourful.

**Serves 6**

**For the soup**

About 1kg winter squash, peeled, deseeded and cut into chunks

2 onions, cut into quarters

Extra virgin olive oil

700ml hot vegetable stock

150ml double cream

Sea salt and freshly ground black pepper

**For the pistou**

3 garlic cloves, peeled

½ teaspoon salt

1 large bunch of basil

6 tablespoons extra virgin olive oil

75g Parmesan cheese, finely grated

**To finish**

A handful of freshly toasted pumpkin seeds

1. Preheat your oven to 190°C/gas mark 5.

2. Place the squash and onions into a roasting tin, pour enough oil to coat them and roast for 40–50 minutes or until soft and caramelised. Transfer to a large saucepan, add the vegetable stock, and liquidize with a hand-held electric blender. Bring to the boil, remove from the heat and add the cream and some salt and pepper to taste.

3. Blend all of the pistou ingredients in a food-processor, or pound them with a pestle and mortar for a rougher texture: garlic and salt first, then basil, a little at a time, then finally the olive oil and cheese.

4. Reheat the soup just before serving but without bringing it to the boil. Pour into bowls, trickle on a little pistou and sprinkle with the pumpkin seeds.

# Triple sunflower salad

A golden, summer-into-autumn salad to celebrate the sunflower. 'Triple' because it contains roasted Jerusalem artichoke roots – a type of perennial sunflower – and is garlanded in toasted sunflower seeds with dollops of roasted sunflower seed butter turned savoury with smoked salt. Don't worry if you can't get hold of this, go for normal salt and blend in a little roasted garlic instead. If you have a few sunflower petals to hand, why not throw them on as well, they are perfectly edible and very pretty.

**Serves 4**

300g Jerusalem artichokes, scrubbed and chopped into chunks

300g sweet potatoes, peeled and cut into thick rounds

300g multicoloured heritage carrots, peeled and sliced in half lengthways

3 red onions, peeled and quartered

Extra virgin olive oil, for roasting, grilling and frying

Sea salt and freshly ground black pepper

8 garlic cloves, peeled

2 ears of sweetcorn

2 thick slices sourdough bread, cut into chunky cubes

A handful of parsley, chopped

Sunflower petals

2 teaspoons walnut oil

Juice of ½ lemon

**For the sunflower seed butter**

550g sunflower seeds

1 tablespoon light olive oil

1 teaspoon smoked salt

1. You can make the sunflower seed butter any time. Preheat your oven to 160°C/gas mark 3. Lay the seeds on a baking tray, place in the oven and toast, stirring occasionally, for about 15 minutes or until light brown. Let them cool, then tip into a food-processor. The seeds will turn first grainy, then flour-like, before finally clumping together. At this point pour in the oil and the salt and keep on blending. The butter will get smoother and smoother the longer you go on. Taste it and adjust the seasoning if you need to, then store the butter in a sterilised jar until you need it.

2. Preheat your oven to 190°C/gas mark 5. Put the artichokes, sweet potatoes, carrots and onions into a large baking tray, pour on enough oil to coat them, and season. Roast for 40–50 minutes, turning occasionally, until soft with caramelized edges. Throw the garlic in for the last 10 minutes, turning the cloves in the oil so that they are coated first.

3. Meanwhile, coat the sweetcorn with a little oil and grill under a high heat, turning occasionally, until they look well toasted, then remove, cool, and slice the kernels onto a plate.

4. In a frying pan, heat a little oil until hot, quickly fry the bread until crispy, then remove onto kitchen paper. Arrange the roasted vegetables on a big serving plate, nestle some spoonfuls of sunflower seed butter between them, then add the sweetcorn kernels, croutons, parsley and sunflower petals.

5. If there is any oil left in the baking tray, tip it into a jar and add the walnut oil and the lemon juice and a little salt and pepper; if there's no oil left, use a little extra virgin olive oil. Shake it up and pour over the salad. Serve while warm.

# Garden granola

Use this as a basic template for granola and mix in whatever seeds and nuts you have to hand – and some dried fruit, too. I have kept mine very simple, limited to the nuts and seeds that I can gather from my garden. Of course, you can eat granola with whatever combination of dairy and fruit you fancy, but I do recommend trying frozen berries: they are like healthy ice lollies.

**Serves 6**

160g raspberries

160g blackberries

200ml honey

100g salted butter

250g porridge oats

100g almonds, roughly chopped

50g pumpkin seeds

50g sunflower seeds

Cold milk and Greek yogurt, to serve

1. Spread the raspberries and blackberries onto a baking tray so that they are not touching each other, then place them in the freezer overnight. Once they are frozen they can be bundled into a plastic freezer bag and removed as you want them.

2. Preheat the oven to 180°C/gas mark 4. Melt the honey and butter together in a large saucepan over a gentle heat and tip in the oats, almonds and seeds. Stir until everything is well coated and then tip onto a baking tray lined with baking paper. Press everything down lightly, then bake for 15–18 minutes or until golden brown. Leave to cool completely.

3. Once cool, break the granola up into chunks and store in an airtight container until needed. Serve with cold milk and Greek yogurt, and a handful of frozen berries.

# Poppy seed rugelach

There are a good many pastries and cakes that make use of dense, nutty poppy seed butter, all of Eastern European origin. Rugelach are traditional Jewish pastries made with a cream-cheese dough and all sorts of different fillings – poppy seed being one. I think they are beautiful, and I particularly like the little black stripes left by the poppy seed butter.

**Makes 48 tiny pastries**

225g cream cheese, at room temperature

225g salted butter, softened

30g caster sugar

Finely grated zest of 1 lemon

1 teaspoon vanilla essence

Pinch of salt

275g plain flour, plus extra for dusting

Poppy seed butter (see page 172)

1 egg

1 tablespoon full-fat milk

Icing sugar, to dust

1. In a large bowl, cream together the cream cheese, butter, sugar, lemon zest, vanilla essence and salt until light and fluffy. Sift in the flour then fold it in with a wooden spoon until just combined into a rough dough. Knead briefly, divide into four portions, wrap each in clingfilm and chill for 1 hour.

2. One at a time, take the portions out of the fridge and roll them out into a 23cm circle, using a little flour to prevent sticking. Spread the surface with a couple of tablespoons of poppy seed butter, not quite to the edges, then use a sharp knife to cut the circle into 12 segments. Roll up each segment from the wide end and place them on a baking tray covered with baking paper. Chill for 45 minutes.

3. Preheat the oven to 180°C/gas mark 4. Whisk together the egg and milk, remove the rugelach from the fridge and brush their tops with this glaze mix. Bake for 15–20 minutes, until golden brown. Remove from the oven and allow to cool on a wire rack. Sift a little icing sugar over the rugelach before serving with coffee.

# Butters

The most obvious ingredients to make into butters are nuts and the bigger seeds. They have the oil within them, and the bulk, and when ground will turn first into crumbs, then into flour, next into something vaguely dough-like, and finally into a smooth and spreadable butter. You just have to hold your nerve and keep your finger on the button.

If you are making your own butters you can play around with additional flavours. Walnut with a little maple syrup (5) makes a gloriously autumnal and moodily sweet spread. Sunflower butter (3) takes well to a touch of vanilla or a little honey. Hazelnut and chocolate is the classic sweet Italian nut butter, *gianduja* (2). Toast 300g of blanched hazelnuts in the oven for 10 minutes, leave to cool, then whizz in a food-processor until they turn into a paste. Meanwhile, melt 200g each of dark and milk chocolate over a double boiler. Add 30g icing sugar, 2 tablespoons hazelnut oil, 2 tablespoons double cream and the chocolate to the food-processor and blend again. Leave it chunky or whizz until smooth, then spoon into sterilised jars. It isn't just sweet additions that you can make to the nut and seed butters: try a little fennel seed in your pumpkin seed butter, smoked salt in your sunflower seed butter or rosemary in your almond butter.

The tiny seeds of poppies are traditionally made into a sweet and nutty filling widely known as poppy seed butter (1), despite the fact that it is in fact a very densely seeded custard. Use it in Russian and Eastern European pastries or just slathered on bread. Pour 225g poppy seeds into a food-processor or coffee grinder (this will have to be in batches, but it can work better than a food-processor, as the seeds are so small) and grind until they start to stick together. Heat 225ml milk with 110g butter and 150g sugar in a pan until the butter has melted and the sugar has dissolved. Whisk 2 eggs in a bowl, then pour a little of the warm milk into it and whisk quickly. Add a little more milk and whisk again. When you have added half the milk, pour the milk and egg mixture back into the rest of the milk in the pan and stir. Heat gently, stirring all the time, until the mixture thickens and you can draw a clear line through the custard as it coats the back of a wooden spoon. Tip in the poppy seeds and stir until well mixed, then pour into sterilised jars and seal. The mixture thickens up as it cools.

Finally, there are many garden treasures that you can mix into real butter to make it more beautiful and delicious: chive flower butter to melt onto freshly barbecued corn on the cob; calendula flower butter to give a golden sheen to a squash risotto; a mixed edible flower, garlic and herb butter (4) to melt into a baked potato. Put a pat of soft butter into a large bowl, then scatter on petals, herbs and maybe garlic salt if it is unsalted butter, and use a wooden spoon to mix all together well. Spoon into ramekins and chill to set, removing it from the fridge 10 minutes before you need it. Or roll the butter into a log in a piece of baking paper and freeze it – this way you can slice off a piece whenever you want something to spread on hot toast.

# Index

# Acknowledgements

Thank you to Jan Billington at Maddocks Farm Organics (www.maddocksfarmorganics.co.uk) in Devon, for the supply of endless perfect, organic, edible flowers, plus the hugely generous loan of such a wonderful space in which to cook and photograph them. This would not be such a good-looking book without your help.

Thanks to Mark Botright at South West Garlic Farm (www.southwestgarlicfarm.co.uk) for the supply of garlic scapes, and to Michael Marriott of David Austin Roses (www.davidaustinroses.co.uk) for roses and rose advice. Pam Lloyd PR were wonderfully helpful in providing ingredients and allowing regular rummaging in their props cupboard, and Ellen Hughes, Claire Thomson, Juliet Roberts and my mum Cath Read all regularly loaned useful things. Thank you all so much. I consider myself very lucky to have been able to pick the excellent and food-obsessed brains of Matt Williamson, Claire Thomson and Mark Diacono along the way and I thank you all for your thoughts, ideas and encouragement.

Three people have made this book the beautiful thing it is: Mark Diacono's photographs are luminous, as ever, all about the food and the light and never about the fork; Matt Cox created a gorgeous, calm and classy design which translates my vision for the book in ways I could never have even quite articulated; and Tatiana Boyko's illustrations make my heart sing. Thank you all.

Thanks to all at Kyle Books, in particular Kyle Cathie and my editor Judith Hannam for spotting the potential in the idea and for guiding it through the process to produce such a fine thing. And to Helena Caldon for her sensitive copy editing.

Last but never least: thanks to Michael, Rowan and Meg, for the eating and the enthusiasm, and for not complaining when I twice packed up half the kitchen and took it off to Devon. And just because.

First published in Great Britain in 2016 by Kyle Books, an imprint of Kyle Cathie Ltd.
192–198 Vauxhall Bridge Road
London SW1V 1DX
general.enquiries@kylebooks.com
www.kylebooks.com

10 9 8 7 6 5 4 3 2 1

ISBN 978 0 85783 343 3

Text © 2016 Lia Leendertz
Design © 2016 Kyle Books
Photographs © 2016 Mark Diacono
Illustrations © 2016 Tatiana Boyko

Lia Leendertz is hereby identified as the author of this work in accordance with Section 77 of the Copyright, Designs and Patents Act 1988.

Editor: Judith Hannam
Editorial assistant: Hannah Coughlin
Designer: Matt Cox at Newman and Eastwood
Photographer: Mark Diacono
Food and prop stylist: Lia Leendertz
Production: Gemma John and Nic Jones

A Cataloguing in Publication record for this title is available from the British Library.

Colour reproduction by F1, London
Printed and bound in China by
C&C Offset Printing Co. Ltd